Uncovering Student Thinking
About **Mathematics**
in the **Common Core**

Grades 6–8

To my grandmother, Hazel Gangi, for inspiring in me the
love of teaching and my former teacher, Helen Cogswell,
for igniting my love of mathematics.

—Cheryl

To those who are faithful in using their passion for mathematics,
love of learning, and hearts of gold to serve kids of all ages, and to my dear
lifelong friend Darwin Ziegelmann who never fails to check in on me
when I need it most.

—Carolyn

Uncovering Student Thinking
About **Mathematics**
in the **Common Core**

Grades 6–8

25
Formative
Assessment
Probes

Cheryl Rose Tobey
Carolyn B. Arline

CORWIN
A SAGE Company

CORWIN
A SAGE Company

FOR INFORMATION:

Corwin
A SAGE Company
2455 Teller Road
Thousand Oaks, California 91320
(800) 233-9936
www.corwin.com

SAGE Publications Ltd.
1 Oliver's Yard
55 City Road
London EC1Y 1SP
United Kingdom

SAGE Publications India Pvt. Ltd.
B 1/I 1 Mohan Cooperative Industrial Area
Mathura Road, New Delhi 110 044
India

SAGE Publications Asia-Pacific Pte. Ltd.
3 Church Street
#10-04 Samsung Hub
Singapore 049483

Acquisitions Editor: Jessica Allan
Associate Editor: Kimberly Greenberg
Editorial Assistant: Heidi Arndt
Production Editor: Melanie Birdsall
Copy Editor: Alison Hope
Typesetter: C&M Digitals (P) Ltd.
Proofreader: Theresa Kay
Indexer: Molly Hall
Cover Designer: Anupama Krishnan

Printed in the United States of America

Library of Congress Cataloging-in-Publication Data

Tobey, Cheryl Rose, author.

Uncovering student thinking about mathematics in the common core, grades 6-8: 25 formative assessment probes/ Cheryl Rose Tobey, Carolyn B. Arline.

pages cm
Includes bibliographical references and index.

ISBN 978-1-4522-3088-7 (pbk.)

1. Mathematics—Study and teaching (Middle school) 2. Mathematical ability—Evaluation. 3. Individualized instruction. 4. Effective teaching. I. Arline, Carolyn, author. II. Title.

QA135.6.T588 2014
510.71'273—dc23   2013024391

This book is printed on acid-free paper.

SUSTAINABLE FORESTRY INITIATIVE
Certified Chain of Custody
Promoting Sustainable Forestry
www.sfiprogram.org
SFI-01268
SFI label applies to text stock

13 14 15 16 17 10 9 8 7 6 5 4 3 2 1

Contents

Preface

Mathematics Assessment Probes

OVERVIEW

Formative assessment informs instruction and supports learning through varying methods and strategies aimed at determining students' prior knowledge of a learning target and using that information to drive instruction that supports each student in moving toward understanding of the learning target. Questioning, observation, and student self-assessment are examples of instructional strategies educators can incorporate to gain insight into student understanding. These instructional strategies become *formative assessments* if the results are used to plan and implement learning activities designed specifically to address the specific needs of the students.

This book focuses on using short sets of diagnostic questions, called Mathematics Assessment Probes (Probes). The Probes are designed to elicit prior understandings and commonly held misunderstandings and misconceptions. This elicitation allows the educator to make sound instructional choices, targeted at a specific mathematics concept and responsive to the specific needs of a particular group of students.

> Diagnostic assessment is as important to teaching as a physical exam is to prescribing an appropriate medical regimen. At the outset of any unit of study, certain students are likely to have already mastered some of the skills that the teacher is about to introduce, and others may already understand key concepts. Some students are likely to be deficient in prerequisite skills or harbor misconceptions. Armed with this diagnostic information, a teacher gains greater insight into what to teach. (McTighe & O'Connor, 2005)

The Mathematics Assessment Probes provided here are tools that enable school teachers in Grades 6 through 8 to gather important insights in a practical way, and that provide immediate information for planning purposes.

AUDIENCE

The first collection of Mathematics Assessment Probes and the accompanying Teacher Notes were written for the busy classroom teacher eager for thoughtful, research-based diagnostic assessments focused on learning difficulties and aimed at enhancing the effectiveness of mathematics instruction. Since the publication of the first three *Uncovering Student Thinking in Mathematics Resources* (Rose & Arline, 2009; Rose, Minton, & Arline, 2007; Rose Tobey & Minton, 2011), we have continually received requests for additional Probes. Both teachers and education leaders have communicated the need for a collection of research-based Probes that focus on narrower grade spans. As well as additional Probes for each grade span, educators were eager for an alignment of the Probes to the Common Core Mathematics Standards (Council of Chief State School Officers [CCSSO], 2010). In response to these requests, we set to work writing, piloting, and field-testing a more extensive set of Probes for middle school teachers with a focus on targeting mathematics concepts within the new standards. This book is one in a series of *Uncovering* resources for the K–2, 3–5, 6–8, and 9–12 grade spans.

ORGANIZATION

This book is organized to provide readers with the purpose, structure, and development of the Mathematics Assessment Probes as well as to support the use of applicable research and instructional strategies in mathematics classrooms.

Chapter 1 provides in-depth information about the process and design of the Mathematics Assessment Probes, and develops an action-research structure we refer to as a QUEST Cycle. Chapters 2 through 6 contain the collection of Probes categorized by concept strands with accompanying Teacher Notes to provide the specific research and instructional strategies for addressing students' challenges with mathematics. Chapter 7 highlights instructional considerations and images from practice to illuminate how easily and in how many varied ways the Probes can be used in mathematics classrooms. This chapter also highlights how use of the Probes can support students' proficiency with the Common Core's Mathematical Practices.

Acknowledgments

We would like to thank the many mathematics educators who during attendance at various professional development sessions gave valuable feedback about features of the Probes, including structures, concepts to target, and purposes of use.

We especially would like to acknowledge the contributions of the following educators who provided ideas and field-tested Probes, gave feedback on Teacher Notes, scheduled classroom visits, and/or opened their classrooms to us to try Probes or interview students: John Aresta, Lisa Beede, Joelle Drake, Michael Dyer, Judy Forrest, Tracey Harnett, Renee Henry, Tracy Kinney, Tom Light, Guy Meader, Judy Morgan, Sandra Roderick, Pamela Rodriquez, Joan Savage, Steven Shaw, Kristin Spangler, Jessica West, Ed Worcester, and the math teachers from Maine's RSU 2.

A very special thanks to Nancy Philbrick and Ruth Wilson for their ongoing support in the piloting of the ideas from this book in their classrooms.

We would like to thank our Corwin editor, Jessica Allan, for her continued support and flexibility, and Page Keeley, our science colleague, who designed the process for developing diagnostic assessment Probes and who tirelessly promotes the use of these assessments for formative assessment purposes, helping to disseminate our work in her travels.

Mostly, we are grateful for the continued support, sacrifice, and patience shown by our families—Corey, Grandad, Carly, Jimmy, Bobby, Samantha, and Jack; and Liz, Kate, Adam, Sophie, and Gram—throughout the writing of this book.

PUBLISHER'S ACKNOWLEDGMENTS

Corwin gratefully acknowledges the contributions of the following reviewers:

Frederika Reisman
Professor and Director,
    Drexel-Torrance Center for
    Creativity and Innovation
Goodwin College,
    Drexel University
Philadelphia, PA

Debra A. Scarpelli
Middle School Mathematics
    Teacher
North Smithfield, RI

About the Authors

Cheryl Rose Tobey is a senior mathematics associate at Education Development Center (EDC) in Massachusetts. She is the project director for Formative Assessment in the Mathematics Classroom: Engaging Teachers and Students (FACETS) and a mathematics specialist for Differentiated Professional Development: Building Mathematics Knowledge for Teaching Struggling Students (DPD); both projects are funded by the National Science Foundation (NSF). She also serves as a director of development for an Institute for Educational Science (IES) project, Eliciting Mathematics Misconceptions (EM2). Her work is primarily in the areas of formative assessment and professional development.

Prior to joining EDC, Tobey was the senior program director for mathematics at the Maine Mathematics and Science Alliance (MMSA), where she served as the co–principal investigator of the mathematics section of the NSF-funded Curriculum Topic Study, and principal investigator and project director of two Title IIa state Mathematics and Science Partnership projects. Prior to working on these projects, Tobey was the co–principal investigator and project director for MMSA's NSF-funded Local Systemic Change Initiative, Broadening Educational Access to Mathematics in Maine (BEAMM), and she was a fellow in Cohort 4 of the National Academy for Science and Mathematics Education Leadership. She is the coauthor of six published Corwin books, including three prior books in the *Uncovering Student Thinking* series (2007, 2009, 2011), two *Mathematics Curriculum Topic Study* resources (2006, 2012), and *Mathematics Formative Assessment: 75 Practical Strategies for Linking Assessment, Instruction and Learning* (2011). Before joining MMSA in 2001 to begin working with teachers, Tobey was a high school and middle school mathematics educator for 10 years. She received her BS in secondary mathematics education from the University of Maine at Farmington and her MEd from City University in Seattle. She currently lives in Maine with her husband and blended family of five children.

Carolyn B. Arline is a secondary mathematics educator, currently teaching high school students in Maine. Carolyn also works as a teacher leader in the areas of mathematics professional development, learning communities, assessment, systematic school reform, standards-based teaching, learning and grading, student-centered classrooms, and technology. She has previously worked as a mathematics specialist at the Maine Mathematics and Science Alliance (MMSA) and continues her work with them as a consultant. Carolyn is a fellow of the second cohort group of the Governor's Academy for Science and Mathematics Educators and serves as a mentor teacher with the current cohort. She participated as a mathematics mentor in the NSF-funded Northern New England Co-Mentoring Network (NNECN) and continues her role as a mentor teacher. She serves as a board member of the Association of Teachers of Mathematics in Maine (ATOMIM) and on local curriculum committees. Carolyn received her BS in secondary mathematics education from the University of Maine.

1

Mathematics
Assessment Probes

To differentiate instruction effectively, teachers need diagnostic assessment strategies to gauge their students' prior knowledge and uncover their misunderstandings. By accurately identifying and addressing areas of difficulties, teachers can help their students avoid becoming frustrated and disenchanted with mathematics and can prevent the perception that "some people just aren't good at math." Diagnostic strategies also support instruction that builds on individual students' existing understandings while addressing their identified difficulties. Targeting specific areas of difficulty—for example, the transition from reasoning about whole numbers to understanding numbers that are expressed in relationship to other numbers (decimals and fractions)—enables teachers to perform focused and effective diagnostic assessment (National Research Council [NRC], 2005, p. 310). The Mathematics Assessment Probes in this book allow teachers to target specific areas of difficulty as identified in research on student learning.

The Probes typically include a prompt or question and a series of responses designed specifically to elicit prior understandings and commonly held misunderstandings that may or may not be uncovered during an instructional unit. In the example in Figure 1.1, students are asked to choose from a selection of responses as well as write about how they determined their answer choice.

This combination of selected responses and further explanation helps to guide teachers in making instructional choices based on the specific needs of their students. Since not all Probes follow the same format, we will discuss the varying formats later in this chapter. If you are wondering what other kinds of Probes are included in this book, take a few

Figure 1.1   Example of a Probe

Estimating Quotients

Determine the best estimate.	Explain your choice.
1. **22.5 ÷ 0.54** a. Between 4 and 5 b. Between 40 and 50 c. Between 400 and 500	
2. **0.683 ÷ 1.9** a. Between 0.1 and 0.5 b. Between 10 and 50 c. Between 100 and 500	
3. **8.4 ÷ 0.04** a. Between 0.2 and 0.4 b. Between 20 and 40 c. Between 200 and 400	

moments to review two or three additional Probes from Chapters 2–6 before continuing reading, but we strongly suggest that you return to read the rest of this chapter before beginning to use the Probes with your students.

At this point you may be asking, "What is the difference between Mathematics Assessment Probes and other assessments?" Comprehensive diagnostic assessments such as for Northwest Education Association (NWEA) and Key Math3 (Pearson), as well as the many state- and district-developed assessments, can provide information important for finding entry points and current levels of understanding within a defined progression of learning for a particular mathematics subdomain such as counting and cardinality. Such assessments will continue to play an important

Are you wondering about the Probes? If you are, we suggest reviewing the following Probes as initial examples:

- Best Estimates: Finding Percents, p. 66
- Value of the Inequality, p. 94
- Perimeter and Area, p. 138

role in schools because they allow teachers to get a snapshot of student understanding across multiple subdomains, often at intervals throughout the year, depending on the structure of the assessment.

How are Probes different from these other assessments? Consider the following vignette:

> In an 8th grade classroom, students are engaged in a class discussion to decide whether a given relationship shown in a table, graph or equation is proportional. After using a Card Sort strategy to individually group cards as "Proportional" and "Not Proportional," the teacher encourages the students to develop a list of characteristics that could be used to decide whether a relationship is proportional. As students share their ideas and come to an agreement, the teacher records the characteristic and draws an example and nonexample to further illustrate the idea for each type of representation. He then gives students an opportunity to regroup their cards, using the defining characteristics they have developed as a class. As the students discuss the results of their sorting process, he listens for and encourages students to use the listed characteristics to justify their choices. Throughout the discussion, the class works together to revise the characteristics already listed and to add additional characteristics that were not included in the initial discussion.
>
> —Adapted from Keeley & Rose Tobey, 2011, p. 1

The Probe used in this vignette, the Proportional Relationship Card Sort Probe (Figure 3.4a), serves as a diagnostic assessment at several points during the lesson. The individual elicitation allows the teacher to diagnose students' current understanding; the conversation about characteristics both builds the teacher's understanding of what students are thinking and creates a learning experience for students to further develop their understanding of the characteristics of proportional relationships. The individual time allotted for regrouping the cards allows the teacher to assess whether students are able to integrate this new knowledge with former conceptions or whether additional instruction or intervention is necessary.

Rather than addressing a variety of math concepts, Probes focus on a particular subconcept within a larger mathematical idea. By pinpointing one subconcept, the assessment can be embedded at the lesson level to address conceptions and misconceptions while learning is under way, helping to bridge from diagnostic to formative assessment.

Helping all students build understanding in mathematics is an important and challenging goal. Being aware of student difficulties and the sources of those difficulties, and designing instruction to diminish them, are important steps in achieving this goal (Yetkin, 2003). The process of using a Probe to diagnose student understandings and misunderstandings and then responding with instructional decisions based on the new information is the key to helping students build their mathematical knowledge. Let's take a look at the complete Probe implementation process we call the *QUEST Cycle* (Figure 1.2):

Figure 1.2   Quest Cycle

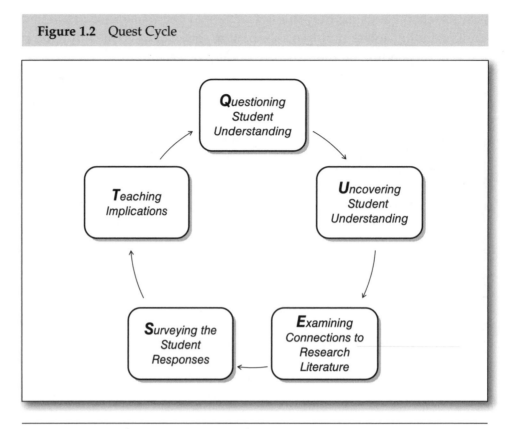

Source: Adapted from Rose, Minton, and Arline (2007).

- **Q**uestioning student understanding: Determine the key mathematical understandings you want students to learn.
- Uncovering student understanding: Use a Probe to uncover understandings and areas of difficulties.
- Examining connections to research and educational literature: Prepare to answer the question, In what ways do your students' understandings relate to those described in the research base?
- Surveying the student responses: Analyze student responses to better understand the various levels of understanding demonstrated in their work.
- Teaching implications: Consider and follow through with next steps to move student learning forward.

Notice that in the Proportional Relationship Card Sort vignette, this cycle is repeated several times within the described instructional period.

The remaining parts of this chapter describe important components of the QUEST Cycle for implementing Probes, including background information on the key mathematics, the structure of the Probes, and connections to the research base. In addition, you will learn how to get started administering the Probes.

QUESTIONING STUDENT UNDERSTANDING: DETERMINE THE KEY MATHEMATICAL CONCEPTS YOU WANT STUDENTS TO LEARN

The Common Core State Standards for Mathematics (referred to as the Common Core or CCSSM) define what students should understand and are the basis of the targeted mathematics concepts addressed by the Probes in this book. These understandings include both conceptual knowledge and procedural knowledge, both of which are important for students' mathematical development.

> Research has strongly established that proficiency in subjects such as mathematics requires conceptual understanding. When students understand mathematics, they are able to use their knowledge flexibly. They combine factual knowledge, procedural facility, and conceptual understanding in powerful ways. (National Council of Teachers of Mathematics [NCTM], 2000, p. 20)

Think about the experience of following step-by-step driving directions to an unfamiliar destination using the commands of a GPS, but never having viewed a road map of the area. Although it may be easy to follow the directions one step at a time, if you lose your satellite reception you will likely not know where to turn next or even which direction to head. Using a GPS without a road map is like learning procedures in math without understanding the concepts behind those procedures. Learners who follow the steps of a mathematical procedure without any conceptual understanding connected to that procedure may get lost when they make a mistake. Understanding the bigger picture enables learners to reason about a solution and/or reconstruct a procedure.

This relationship between understanding concepts and being proficient with procedures is complex. Table 1.1 provides some examples of each type of understanding for a variety of contexts.

The relationship between understanding concepts and being proficient with procedures is further developed in the examples of the Probes that follow. Both conceptual understanding and procedural flexibility are important goals that complement each other in developing strong mathematical abilities. Each is necessary and only together do they become sufficient.

The following examples of Probes will further distinguish conceptual and procedural understandings.

Example 1: Finding Volume Probe

The Finding Volume Probe (see Figure 1.3) is designed to elicit whether students understand the formula numerically and quantitatively (NCTM, 2003, p. 101). Students who correctly determine the volume of the first problem yet choose "c. Not enough information" for the second problem may be able to apply the volume formula, $V = lwh$, when given a length, width, and height, but lack the ability to apply the formula to a varied representation of

Table 1.1   Procedural vs. Conceptual Understanding

Procedural Knowledge	Accompanying Conceptual Understanding	Examples
Learn and apply a series of steps.	• Explain why the steps make sense mathematically. • Use reasoning to rebuild the steps if needed. • Make connections between alternative steps that could be used to find the solution. • Describe the parts of the formula and relate the parts to various models/representations of situations involving use of the formula.	When adding $2\frac{2}{3}$ and $-6\frac{3}{4}$, the student is able to describe and connect two different methods for adding these rational numbers. Can find the volume of rectangle when given the area of the base and height of the figure rather than the length, width, and height.
Find a solution.	• Show flexibility in representing mathematical situations. • Justify whether the answer makes sense (numerical example: reasoning about the size of numbers and a mathematical operation). • Troubleshoot a mistake. • Represent thinking with symbols, models, and/or diagrams.	Without actually calculating, can reason that 35.5 divided by 0.52 must be about 70 since dividing by 0.5 doubles a number. Can sort a collection of geometric shapes by attending to their attributes.
Apply a rule.	• Explain why the rule makes sense mathematically.	Can show or explain why dividing a negative number by a negative number results in a positive number. Can show or explain why the exponents are added (or subtracted) when simplifying expressions with exponents.

the concept. The following student responses to "Explain Your Reasoning" for item 2 are indicative of conceptual understanding of the formula:

- Volume is the area of the base times the height. If you flip this box, then 24 is the base and 4 is the height so 24 cm² * 4 cm is 96 cm³.
- You already have some of the information needed. If you rearrange l * w * h to fit the information given, you would have (l * h) * w. You are given that l * h is 24 cm² and (24 cm²) (4 cm) = 96 cm³.

More information about this Probe can be found on pages 148–153.

Figure 1.3 Finding Volume Probe

Finding Volume

Determine the volume of the figure.	Explain your choice.
1. 4 m 6 m 10 m a. 20 m³ b. 240 m³ c. Not enough information	
2. 24 cm² 4 cm a. 28 cm³ b. 96 cm³ c. Not enough information	
3. 10 m 6 m 8 m a. 480 cm³ b. 240 cm³ c. Not enough information	
4. 40 m² 7 m a. 280 m³ b. 140 m³ c. Not enough information	

Example 2: Is It Positive? Probe

In the Is it Positive? Probe, students with conceptual understanding can make judgments about the sign of the answer without having to do the actual calculations. They understand when the rule "two negatives always makes a positive" appropriately applies and are able to use the order of operations and other properties of operations to help determine whether

Figure 1.4   Is It Positive? Probe

Is It Positive?

Without actually calculating, use reasoning to determine whether the expression results in a POSITIVE answer.

Circle Yes or No.	Explain your choice.
a. $-(-53.4 + 92.3)$ Yes No	
b. $-34.23 - 27.9$ Yes No	
c. $\dfrac{-5.3 - 3.6}{(-3.2)(-4.3)}$ Yes No	
d. $-2.4 - (-3.4 \cdot -6.4)$ Yes No	

the answers will be positive or negative. Students with only a procedural understanding are more likely to calculate to find the answer rather than to reason about the size of the numbers and the properties of operations. More information about this Probe can be found on pages 49–54.

Example 3: Linear Equations Probe

In the Linear Equations Probe, students with conceptual and procedural understanding pay attention to the key features of the graph in

Figure 1.5 Linear Equations Probe

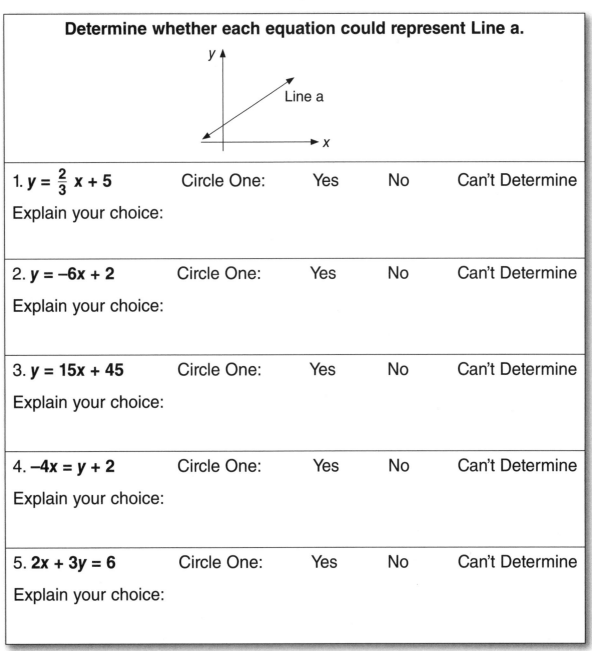

Linear Equations

Determine whether each equation could represent Line a.

1. $y = \frac{2}{3}x + 5$ Circle One: Yes   No   Can't Determine

Explain your choice:

2. $y = -6x + 2$ Circle One: Yes   No   Can't Determine

Explain your choice:

3. $y = 15x + 45$ Circle One: Yes   No   Can't Determine

Explain your choice:

4. $-4x = y + 2$ Circle One: Yes   No   Can't Determine

Explain your choice:

5. $2x + 3y = 6$ Circle One: Yes   No   Can't Determine

Explain your choice:

relationship to the equation. Students with conceptual understanding know that although the scale on the x- and y-axes is unknown, the graph of the line shows a positive y-intercept and rate of change. This information can be determined from each of the equations. More information about this Probe can be found on pages 109–113.

UNCOVERING STUDENT UNDERSTANDING: USE A PROBE TO UNCOVER UNDERSTANDINGS AND AREAS OF DIFFICULTIES

Misunderstandings are likely to develop as a normal part of learning mathematics. These misunderstandings can be classified as conceptual misunderstandings, overgeneralizations, preconceptions, and partial conceptions. These are summarized in Figure 1.6, and each is described in more detail below.

Figure 1.6   Mathematics Assessment Probes

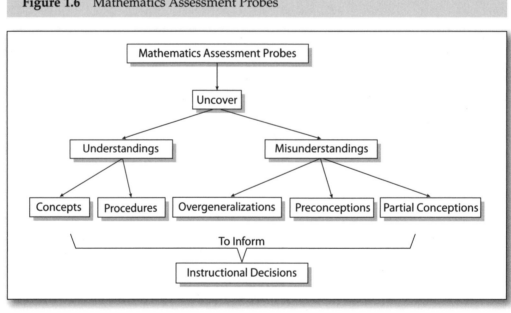

Source: Adapted from Rose, Minton, and Arline (2007).

In *Hispanic and Anglo Students' Misconceptions in Mathematics*, Jose Mestre (1989) summarizes cognitive research as follows: Students do not come to the classroom as "blank slates" (Resnick, 1983). Instead, they come with theories constructed from their everyday experiences. They have actively constructed these theories, an activity crucial to all successful learning. Some of the theories that students use to make sense of the world are, however, incomplete half-truths (Mestre, 1989). They are misconceptions.

Misconceptions are a problem for two reasons. First, when students use them to interpret new experiences, misconceptions interfere with learning. Second, because they have actively constructed them, students are emotionally and intellectually attached to their misconceptions. Even when students recognize that their misconceptions can harm their learning, they are reluctant to let them go. Given this, it is critical that middle school teachers uncover and address their students' misconceptions as early as possible.

For the purposes of this book, misconceptions will be categorized as *overgeneralizations*, *partial conceptions*, and *conceptual misunderstandings*. The following brief summary describes each of these categories of misconception.

- **Overgeneralizations:** Information extended or applied to another context in an inappropriate way. Overgeneralizations include vernacular issues related to differences between the everyday meaning of words and their mathematical meaning.
- **Partial Conceptions:** Hybrids of correct and incorrect ideas. This may result from difficulty generalizing or connecting concepts or distinguishing between two concepts.
- **Conceptual Misunderstandings:** Content students "learned" in school but that has been misinterpreted and internalized; these misunderstandings often go unnoticed by the teacher. Students often make their own meaning out of what is taught. (Adapted from Keeley, 2012)

Table 1.2 provides an example from each of the above categories. The examples provided are from the progressions for the Common Core written by the Common Core Standards Writing Team (2011a, 2011b, 2012).

Some misunderstandings do not fall distinctly into one category but can be characterized in more than one way. For example, the conceptual misunderstanding of the base of a triangle can also be considered to be an overgeneralization. In addition, some misconceptions are more deeply rooted and

Table 1.2   Misconceptions: Categories and Examples

Misconception Category	Example
Overgeneralizations: Information extended or applied to another context in an inappropriate way	"Failure to see juxtaposition as indicating multiplication, e.g., evaluating $3x$ as 35 when $x = 5$, or rewriting $8 - 2a$ as $6a$." The underlying lack of conceptual understanding of the meaning of the expression $3x$ can lead to these common errors, which in this case could be considered overgeneralizations.

(Continued)

(Continued)

Misconception Category	Example
Partial Conception: Hybrids of correct and incorrect ideas. This may result from difficulty generalizing or connecting concepts or distinguishing between two concepts.	"A common error in setting up proportions is placing numbers in incorrect locations. This is especially easy to do when the order in which quantities are stated in the problem is switched within the problem statement." Students have difficulty recognizing how the relationship between the quantities is represented in the equation.
Conceptual Misunderstandings: Content students "learned" in school but that has been misinterpreted and internalized; these misunderstandings often go unnoticed by the teacher. Students often make their own meaning out of what is taught.	"When finding the area of a triangle, students consider the base only by the shown orientation, do not view the height as associated with the chosen base, and/or may forget to take half of the product of the base times the height." At the root of each of these difficulties is the lack of conceptual understanding.

Source: Common Core Standards Writing Team (2011a, 2011b, 2012).

difficult to change than others. It is important to make the distinction between what we might call a silly mistake and a more fundamental one that may be the product of a deep-rooted misunderstanding. In her guest editorial, "Misunderstanding Misconceptions," Page Keeley describes various practitioner misunderstandings related to using the science Probes in the National Science Teachers Association's *Uncovering Student Ideas in Science* series (Keeley, 2012, pp. 12–15). Both in our work with Page and with mathematics educators using the *Uncovering Student Thinking in Mathematics* resources, we have encountered many similar misunderstandings among teachers:

- *All misconceptions are the same.* The word *misconception* is frequently used to describe all ideas students bring to their learning that are not completely accurate. In contrast, researchers often use labels such as *alternative frameworks, naïve ideas, phenomenological primitives, children's ideas,* etc., to imply that these ideas are not completely "wrong" in a student's common-sense world.
- *Misconceptions are a bad thing.* The word *misconception* seems to have a pejorative connotation to most practitioners. According to constructivist theory, when new ideas are encountered, they are either accepted, rejected, or modified to fit existing conceptions. It is the

cognitive dissonance students experience when they realize an existing mental model no longer works for them that makes them willing to give up a preexisting idea in favor of a scientific one. Having ideas to work from, even if they are not completely accurate, leads to deeper understanding when students engage in a conceptual-change process (Watson & Konicek, 1990).

- *All misconceptions are major barriers to learning.* Just as some learning standards have more weight in promoting conceptual learning than others, the same is true of misconceptions. For example, a student may have a misconception for only one type of problem situation (see Figure 1.5 Linear Equations Probe), but can make great strides in learning to model and represent operations for other situations. (Adapted from Keeley, 2012)

To teach in a way that avoids creating any misconceptions is not possible, and we have to accept that students will make some incorrect generalizations that will remain hidden unless the teacher makes specific efforts to uncover them (Askew & Wiliam, 1995). Our job as educators is to minimize the chances of students' harboring misconceptions by knowing the potential difficulties students are likely to encounter, using assessments to elicit misconceptions, and implementing instruction designed to build new and accurate mathematical ideas.

The primary purpose of the Probes is to elicit understandings and areas of difficulties related to specific mathematical ideas. In addition to these content-specific related targets, the Probes also elicit skills and processes related to the Standards for Mathematical Practice, especially those related to the use of reasoning and explanation. If you are unfamiliar with the Standards for Mathematical Practice or would like a refresher, you can find descriptions of them in Appendix A.

WHAT IS THE STRUCTURE OF A PROBE?

The Probes are designed to include two levels of response—one for elicitation of common understandings and misunderstandings, and the other for the elaboration of individual student thinking. Each of the levels is described in more detail below.

Level 1: Answer Response

Since the elicitation level is designed to uncover common understandings and misunderstandings, a structured format using stems, correct answers, and distractors is used to narrow ideas found in the related research. The formats typically fall into one of three categories, shown in Figures 1.7 through 1.9.

Selected Response Probes

- Two or more items are provided, each with one stem (or prompt), one correct answer, and one or more distractors; or
- Two or more separate problems or statements are provided, each with an answer choice needing to be justified.

Figure 1.7   Measures of Center and Spread

Measures of Center and Spread

Mr. Hernandez collected the following information about students' scores on a test that consisted of a total of 100 points:

The median is 84 points.
The mode is 90 points.
The mean is 88 points.

Decide whether the statement is True or False.	Explain your choice.
1. ***More students scored 90 points than any other number of points.*** a. True b. False c. Not enough information	
2. ***At least half the students scored 88 or fewer points.*** a. True b. False c. Not enough information	
3. ***The scores range from 84 to 90.*** a. True b. False c. Not enough information	

Math Talk Probe

- Two or more statements are provided, and students choose the statement they agree with. This format is adapted from *Concept Cartoons in Science Education,* created by Stuart Naylor and Brenda Keogh (2000) for probing student ideas in science.

Figure 1.8 Perimeter and Area

Perimeter and Area

The two rectangles have the same perimeter.

Rectangle A:
    Length = a inches
    Width = b inches
    Perimeter = 40 inches

Rectangle B:
    Length = l inches
    Width = e inches
    Perimeter = 40 inches

Decide if you agree or disagree with each student's statement about the rectangles.

Statement	Explain your choice.
1. *The two rectangles could have different side measures.* **Circle one:** Agree Disagree	
2. *The two rectangles have equivelent area measures.* **Circle one:** Agree Disagree	

Examples and Nonexamples Card Sort Probe

- Several examples and nonexamples are given, and students are asked to sort the items into the correct piles.

Level 2: Explanation of Response Choice

The second level of each of the Probes is designed so students can elaborate on the reasoning they used to respond to the Level 1 elicitation question. Mathematics teachers gain a wealth of information by delving

Figure 1.9 Number Card Sort

Number Card Sort

Rational	Irrational	i. $-\sqrt{9}$	j. $\dfrac{22}{7}$
a. $\sqrt{2}$	b. $\sqrt{25}$	k. $\dfrac{5.3}{7.2}$	l. $(\sqrt{3})(-\sqrt{2})$
c. $\dfrac{1}{3}$	d. Π	m. $\dfrac{0}{4}$	n. $0.8\bar{3}$
e. $\dfrac{5}{0}$	f. $\sqrt{3}\cdot\sqrt{3}$	o. $\dfrac{\sqrt{5}}{\sqrt{3}}$	p. $\dfrac{-8}{\sqrt{7}}$
g. $\sqrt{2}\cdot\sqrt{5}$	h. $\dfrac{10}{9}$		

into the thinking behind students' answers, not just when answers are wrong, but also when they are correct. Although the Level 1 answers and distractors are designed to target common understandings and misunderstandings, the elaboration level allows educators to look more deeply at student thinking. Often a student chooses a specific response, correct or incorrect, for a typical reason. Also, there are many different ways to approach a problem correctly; therefore, the elaboration level allows educators to look for patterns in thinking and in methods used. Chapter 7 delves deeper into expectations for this elaboration and its relationship to the Common Core Mathematical Practices (often shortened to Mathematical Practices).

QUEST CYCLE: STRUCTURE OF THE SUPPORTING TEACHER NOTES

The Teacher Notes included with each Probe have been designed to help you prepare for a QUEST Cycle. The first two components of the cycle, *questioning student understanding* and *uncovering student understanding*, have been described more fully above. We will use the description of the Teacher Notes to provide more details about the remaining components of the cycle.

Questions to Consider About the Key Mathematical Concepts

This section of the Teacher Notes helps to focus a teacher on the key conceptual and procedural mathematics addressed by the particular Probe and gives information about alignment to Common Core standards at a particular grade level. Figure 1.10 shows an example from this section of the Estimating Quotients Teacher Notes.

Figure 1.10 Questions to Consider About the Key Mathematical Concepts

---

When solving problems involving the division of decimals, can students reason about the size of the numbers and the effect of the operation to determine a reasonable estimate? To what extent do they

- reason correctly about the size of the divisor and dividend?
- determine whether the quotient will be smaller or larger than the dividend?
- describe how to use this reasoning to determine an estimate?

(Continued)

(Continued)

Common Core Connection (CCSS.Math.Content.6.NS.B.2 and CCSS.Math.Content.6.NS.B.3)

Grade: Sixth

Domain: The Number System

Cluster:

Compute fluently with multi-digit numbers and find common factors and multiples.

2. Fluently divide multi-digit numbers using the standard algorithm.

3. Fluently add, subtract, multiply, and divide multi-digit decimals using the standard algorithm for each operation.

Uncovering Student Understanding About the Key Concepts

This section of the Teacher Notes (Figure 1.11) breaks down the concepts and ideas described in the "Questioning" section into specific understandings and areas of difficulty targeted by the Probe.

Figure 1.11 Uncovering Student Understanding About the Key Concepts

---

Using the Estimating Quotients Probe can provide the following information about how the students are thinking about the effect of operating with decimals.

Do they

- correctly reason about the size of the dividend and divisor?

- correctly reason about the size of the quotient?

- use reasoning about the size of the decimals and the effect of the division?

Do they

OR • apply incorrect place value thinking?

OR • apply an overgeneralization of "division always results in a smaller answer"?

OR • revert to applying an algorithm rather than using reasoning to determine an estimate?

Exploring Excerpts From Educational Resources and Related Research

This section of the Teacher Notes (Figure 1.12) includes excerpts from cognitive research related to the common areas of difficulty targeted by the

Probe. The excerpts are meant to provide some background from the research base behind the development of the Probe. The references provide an opportunity for you to seek additional information when needed. This research base is an important component in the Probe development process. More information on the origin of the Probe development process can be found in Appendix B.

Figure 1.12   Exploring Excerpts From Educational Resources and Related Research

---

Common areas of difficulty for students:

Multiplying and dividing fractions and decimals can be challenging for many students because of problems that are primarily conceptual rather than procedural. From their experience with whole numbers, many students appear to develop a belief that "multiplication makes bigger and division make smaller." (NCTM, 2000, p. 218)

Errors show that many students have learned rules for manipulating symbols without understanding what those symbols mean or why the rules work. Many students are unable to reason appropriately about symbols for rational numbers and do not have the strategic competence that would allow them to catch their mistakes. (NRC, 2001, p. 234)

Developing fluency requires a balance and connection between conceptual understanding and computational proficiency. Computational methods that are overpracticed without understanding are often forgotten or remembered incorrectly (Hiebert 1999; Kamii, Lewis, and Livingston 1993; Hiebert and Lindquist 1990). (NCTM, 2000, p. 35)

---

*S*urveying the Prompts and Selected Responses in the Probe

This section of the Teacher Notes (Figure 1.13) includes information about the prompt, selected response/answer(s), and distractors. Sample student responses are given for a selected number of elicited understandings and misunderstandings. This initial preparation will help expedite the analysis process once you administer the Probe to students.

Figure 1.13   Surveying the Prompts and Selected Responses in the Probe

---

The Probe consists of three separate selected response items. The prompts and selected responses are designed to elicit understandings and common difficulties as described in the following table:

(Continued)

(Continued)

If a student chooses	It is likely that the student
1b, 2a, 3c (correct answers)	• is correctly reasoning about the size of the decimals and the effect of the operation [See Sample Student Response 1]; or • has correctly applied an algorithm rather than using reasoning to determine an estimate [See Sample Student Response 2]. *Look for indication of the student's understanding in the written explanations of how the student got the answer.*
1a, 2a, 3a	• is applying the incorrect rule of "division makes smaller." Note that applying this rule results in selecting the correct response for #2 [See Sample Student Response 3].
Various other patterns	• inconsistently applies correct reasoning about either the size of the decimal or the effect of the operation; and/or • has incorrectly applied an algorithm [See Sample Student Responses 4 and 5].

Teaching Implications and Considerations

Being aware of student difficulties and their sources is important, but acting on that information to design and provide instruction that will diminish those difficulties is even more important. The information in this section of the Teacher Notes (Figure 1.14) is broken into two categories: (1) ideas for eliciting more information from students about their understanding and difficulties; and (2) ideas for planning instruction in response to what you learned from the results of administering the Probe. Although these ideas are included in the Teacher Notes, we strongly encourage you to pursue additional research-based teaching implications.

Figure 1.14 Teaching Implications and Considerations

Ideas for eliciting more information from students about their understanding and difficulties:

- For students who incorrectly reason about the size of the decimals, ask, "What benchmark or whole number is this number close to?"
- For students who apply the "division makes smaller" rule ask, "How can you model 2 divided by 0.5?" If they are able to correctly show that there are 4 "halves" in 2, follow up with, "How can this help you think about these problems?"
- For students who apply an algorithm rather than estimating, ask, "How might you think about this without actually calculating an answer?"

Ideas for planning instruction in response to what you learned from the results of administering the Probe:

- Use representations and concrete models such as number lines and base-ten blocks to help students understand division as how many ___ in ___.
- Provide a problem context from which students can make sense of the results.

- Focus on the meaning of the operation before introducing steps of an algorithm.
- Continue to require students to reason about the size of the numbers and the effect of the operation to determine an estimate as a method of checking for the reasonableness of the results of applying an algorithm.

Included in the Teaching section of the Teacher Notes are sample student responses; examples of these are shown in Figure 1.15.

Figure 1.15 Sample Student Responses to Division Estimates

Responses That Suggest Understanding

Sample Student Response 1

Probe Item 1. b. If you have 20 and you want to know how many .5's go into 20, it will double it. Takes two .5 for every 1. That means it is about 40.

Probe Item 2. a. If you have about .5 and want to know how many 2's go into .5 then it can't even be 1.

Probe Item 3. c. If you have about 8 and divide into really small amounts like pennies then it would be a lot. 4 pennies in $1 is 25. 8 of these would be 200.

Sample Student Response 2

Probe Item 1. b. I rounded .54 to 50 and moved the decimal. $50\overline{)2250}$. 45 is between 40 and 50.

Responses That Suggest Difficulty

Sample Student Response 3

Probe Item 3. b. I am thinking between 20 and 40 makes sense. 8 ÷ 4 is 2 but you are talking about decimals here.

Sample Student Response 4

Probe Item 2. a. 0.683 rounds to 1 and 1.9 rounds to 2. 1 ÷ 2 is 2. None of the answers work but since I rounded I will pick *a* since it is closest to 2.

Sample Student Response 5

Probe Item 3. b. Estimate then divide, move the decimals to divide. $4\overline{)80}$.

Variations

For some Probes, adaptations and variations are provided and can be found following the Teacher Notes and sample student responses to the Probe. A variation of a Probe provides an alternative structure (selected response, multiple selections, opposing views, or examples/nonexamples) for the question within the same grade span. In contrast, an adaptation to a Probe is similar in content to the original, but the level of mathematics is changed for a different grade span.

Action Research Reflection Template

A Reflection Template is included in Appendix C. The Reflection Template provides a structured approach to working through the QUEST Cycle with a Probe. The components of the template are described in Figure 1.16.

Figure 1.16   Reflection Template

Questions to Consider About the Key Mathematical Concepts

What is the concept you wish to target? Is the concept at grade level or is it a prerequisite?

Uncovering Student Understanding About the Key Concepts

How will you collect information from students (e.g., paper and pencil, interview, student response system, etc.)? What form will you use (e.g., one-page Probe, card sort, etc.)? Are there adaptations you plan to make? Review the summary of typical student responses.

Exploring Excerpts From Educational Resources and Related Research

Review the quotes from research about common difficulties related to the Probe. What do you predict to be common understandings and/or misunderstandings for your students?

Surveying the Prompts and Selected Responses in the Probe

Sort by selected responses and then re-sort by trends in thinking. What common understandings/misunderstandings did the Probe elicit? How do these elicited understandings/misunderstandings compare to those listed in the Teacher Notes?

Teaching Implications and Considerations

Review the bulleted list and decide how you will take action. What actions did you take? How did you assess the impact of those actions? What are your next steps?

BEGINNING TO USE THE PROBES

Now that you have a background on the design of the Probes, the accompanying Teacher Notes, and the QUEST Cycle, it is time to think about how to get started using the Probes with your students.

Choosing a Probe: Determining which Probe to use depends on a number of factors, including time of year, alignment to curriculum, and range of abilities within your classroom. We recommend you spend some time reviewing the Probes at your grade level first but also that you make note of additional Probes that may be appropriate for your students.

Deciding How to Administer a Probe: Depending on your purpose, Probes can be given to one student or to all students in your classroom. You may wish to give a Probe to only one student (or several) if you notice the student or group is struggling with a related concept. By giving a Probe to all students, you can gain a sense of patterns of understanding and difficulty in order to target instruction. Although all Probes can be given as a written explanation, we encourage you to use the Probes as interview prompts in order to Probe their thinking even further. Using the Probes in interviews is described in more detail in Chapter 7.

Talking With Students About Probes: Probes are not meant to be graded! We have found that students "buy into" the diagnostic nature of the Probes, especially if the process is shared explicitly with them. Talk to your students about the importance of explaining their thinking in mathematics and why you will ask additional questions to understand more about their thinking.

When giving a Probe, be sure to read through the directions out loud, repeating them as necessary. Do not try to correct students on the spot; instead, ask additional probing questions to determine whether the additional questions prompt the student to think differently. If not, do not stop to try to teach the students "in the moment." Instead, take in the information and think about the next appropriate instructional steps. If students are having difficulty, reassure them that you will be working with them to learn more about the content in the Probe.

HOW TO NAVIGATE THE BOOK

This chapter provided the background information needed to begin to dig into the Probes and think about how you will use them with your students. The next five chapters include 25 sets of Probes and accompanying Teacher Notes, and the final chapter includes additional considerations for using the Probes.

Chapters 2 Through 6: The Probes

Table 1.3 provides an "at-a-glance" look of the targeted grade span and related domain of the content of the 25 Probes.

Table 1.3 Mathematics Assessment Probes

		Grade 6	
Chapter	Page Numbers	Probe	CCSS Domain
2	28	Estimating Quotients	The Number System
2	33	Division of Fractions	The Number System
2	38	Number Lines	The Number System
3	66	Best Estimates: Finding Percents	Ratios and Proportional Relationships
3	71	Comparing Measures	Ratios and Proportional Relationships
5	121	Measures of Center and Spread	Statistics and Probability
6	138	Perimeter and Area	Geometry
		Grade 7	
2	43	Rational Number Multiplication Estimates	The Number System
2	49	Is It Positive?	The Number System
3	75	Best Estimates: Solving Proportions	Ratios and Proportional Relationships
3	80	Proportional Reasoning Sort	Ratios and Proportional Relationships
4	94	Value of the Inequality	Expressions and Equations
4	100	Writing Equations	Expressions and Equations
5	126	What's the Chance?	Statistics and Probability
6	148	Finding Volume	Geometry
6	154	Scale	Geometry
6	169	Parallelograms	Geometry
		Grade 8	
2	55	Number Card Sort	The Number System
4	105	Is It Equivalent?	Expressions and Equations
4	109	Linear Equations	Functions
4	114	Is It a Linear Function?	Functions
5	131	Scatterplots	Statistics and Probability
6	143	Properties of Angles	Geometry
6	159	Right Triangles	Geometry
6	164	Heights of Solids	Geometry

The beginning of each Probe chapter (Chapters 2–6) includes background on the development of the Probes to align with the relevant Common Core domain and standards and a summary chart to guide your review and selection of Probes and variations to use with your students.

Chapter 7: Additional Considerations

The QUEST Cycle components are explained in detail within this chapter as well as for each specific Probe through the accompanying Teacher Notes. In addition to these ideas that are specific to the Probe are instructional considerations that cut across the Probes. Such considerations include ways to use the Probes over time to promote mathematical discussions, to support and assess students' ability to provide justification, and to promote conceptual change.

We recommend that you scan the contents of Chapter 7 before beginning to use the Probes, but that you not try to "do it all" the first time out. After using the Probes, return to Chapter 7 to pinpoint one or two considerations to implement and try out those ideas before returning to consider implementing additional ideas.

FINAL CHAPTER 1 THOUGHTS

We hope these Probes will support you in your work in trying to uncover your students' thinking and understanding and will inspire you to explore ways to respond to their strengths and difficulties in order to move students' learning forward.

2

Number System Probes

The content of the Probes in this chapter aligns with the standards for Grades 6 through 8. The Probes and their variations will also be relevant beyond the aligned grade level for students in higher grades who have not yet met standards from previous grade levels as well as for students who have already met the standards at their own grade level.

We developed these Probes to address this critical area of focus for middle school students, described in the standards (CCSSO, 2010) as follows:

> The content of the Probes in this chapter aligns with the standards for Grades 6 through 8. The Probes and their variations will also be relevant beyond the aligned grade level for students in higher grades who have not yet met standards from previous grade levels as well as for students who have already met the standards at their own grade level.

- Apply and extend previous understandings of multiplication and division to divide fractions by fractions.
- Compute fluently with multi-digit numbers and find common factors and multiples.
- Apply and extend previous understandings of numbers to the system of rational numbers.
- Apply and extend previous understandings of operations with fractions to add, subtract, multiply, and divide rational numbers.
- Know that there are numbers that are not rational, and approximate them with rational numbers.

Common Core Math Content

Common Core Mathematical Content	Related Question	Probe Name
Fluently divide multi-digit numbers using the standard algorithm. CCSS.Math.Content.6.NS.B.2	When solving problems involving the division of decimals, can students reason about the size of the numbers and the effect of the operation to determine a reasonable estimate?	Estimating Quotients (p. 28)
Interpret and compute quotients of fractions, and solve word problems involving division of fractions by fractions. CCSS.Math.Content.6.NS.A.1	When solving problems that model division with fractions, can students relate a given model to the numerical expression it represents?	Division of Fractions (p. 33)
Understand a rational number as a point on the number line. CCSS.Math.Content.6.NS.C.6	When locating a fraction on the number line, can students determine the whole and the size of the intervals to correctly name a point?	Number Lines (p. 38)
Apply and extend previous understandings of multiplication and division and of fractions to multiply and divide rational numbers. CCSS.Math.Content.7.NS.A.2	When estimating the products of rational numbers, can students reason about the size and sign of the numbers and the effect of the operation?	Rational Number Multiplication Estimates (p. 43) Variation: Rational Number Division Estimates (p. 48)
Apply and extend previous understandings of addition and subtraction to add and subtract rational numbers. CCSS.Math.Content.7.NS.A.1	When solving computation problems involving positive and negative numbers, can students reason whether the results are positive?	Is It Positive? (p. 49) Variation: Are You Positive? (p. 54)
Know that numbers that are not rational are called irrational. CCSS.Math.Content.8.NS.A.1	When classifying numbers, can students determine whether a number is a rational or irrational number, or whether the result of computing two numbers will result in a rational or irrational number?	Number Card Sort (p. 55) Variation: Is It Irrational? (p. 63)

Take a look at the variations that are available with some of the Probes in this chapter. All of these variations address number system ideas but may extend the idea or offer a different structure for administering them. When available, variation Probes follow the Teacher Notes and associated reproducibles for the related original Probe.

Estimating Quotients

Determine the best estimate.	Explain your choice.
1. **22.5 ÷ 0.54** a. Between 4 and 5 b. Between 40 and 50 c. Between 400 and 500	
2. **0.683 ÷ 1.9** a. Between 0.1 and 0.5 b. Between 10 and 50 c. Between 100 and 500	
3. **8.4 ÷ 0.04** a. Between 0.2 and 0.4 b. Between 20 and 40 c. Between 200 and 400	

Teacher Notes: Estimating Quotients

Questions to Consider About the Key Mathematical Concepts

When solving problems involving the division of decimals, can students reason about the size of the numbers and the effect of the operation to determine a reasonable estimate? To what extent do they

- reason correctly about the size of the divisor and dividend?
- determine whether the quotient will be smaller or larger than the dividend?
- describe how to use this reasoning to determine an estimate?

Common Core Connection (CCSS.Math.Content.6.NS.B.2 and CCSS.Math. Content.6.NS.B.3)

Grade: Sixth

Domain: The Number System

Cluster:

Compute fluently with multi-digit numbers and find common factors and multiples.

2. Fluently divide multi-digit numbers using the standard algorithm.

3. Fluently add, subtract, multiply, and divide multi-digit decimals using the standard algorithm for each operation.

Uncovering Student Understanding About the Key Concepts

Using the Estimating Quotients Probe can provide the following information about how the students are thinking about the effect of operating with decimals.

Do they

- correctly reason about the size of the dividend and divisor?

OR

Do they

- apply incorrect place value thinking?

- correctly reason about the size of the quotient?

OR

- apply an overgeneralization of "division always results in a smaller answer"?

- use reasoning about the size of the decimals and the effect of the division?

OR

- revert to applying an algorithm rather than using reasoning to determine an estimate?

Exploring Excerpts From Educational Resources and Related Research

Common areas of difficulty for students:

Multiplying and dividing fractions and decimals can be challenging for many students because of problems that are primarily conceptual rather than procedural. From their experience with whole numbers, many students appear to develop a belief that "multiplication makes bigger and division make smaller." (NCTM, 2000, p. 218)

Errors show that many students have learned rules for manipulating symbols without understanding what those symbols mean or why the rules work. Many students are unable to reason appropriately about symbols for rational numbers and do not have the strategic competence that would allow them to catch their mistakes. (NRC, 2001, p. 234)

Developing fluency requires a balance and connection between conceptual understanding and computational proficiency. Computational methods that are overpracticed without under-standing are often forgotten or remembered incorrectly (Hiebert 1999; Kamii, Lewis, and Livingston 1993; Hiebert and Lindquist 1990). (NCTM, 2000, p. 35)

Surveying the Prompts and Selected Responses in the Probe

The Probe consists of three separate selected response items. The prompts and selected responses are designed to elicit understandings and common difficulties as described the following table.

If a student chooses	It is likely that the student
1b, 2a, 3c (correct answers)	• is correctly reasoning about the size of the decimals and the effect of the operation [See Sample Student Response 1]; or • has correctly applied an algorithm rather than using reasoning to determine an estimate [See Sample Student Response 2]. *Look for indication of the student's understanding in the written explanations of how the student got the answer.*
1a, 3a	• is applying the incorrect rule of "division makes smaller." Note that applying this rule results in selecting the correct response, 2a, for #2 [See Sample Student Response 3].
Various other patterns	• inconsistently applies correct reasoning about either the size of the decimal or the effect of the operation; and/or • has incorrectly applied an algorithm [See Sample Student Responses 4 and 5].

Teaching Implications and Considerations

Ideas for eliciting more information from students about their understanding and difficulties:

- For students who incorrectly reason about the size of the decimals, ask, "What benchmark or whole number is this number close to?"
- For students who apply the "division makes smaller" rule, ask, "How can you model 2 divided by 0.5?" If they are able to correctly show that there are 4 "halves" in 2, follow up with, "How can this help you think about the problems?"
- For students who apply an algorithm rather than estimating, ask, "How might you think about this without actually calculating an answer?"

Ideas for planning instruction in response to what you learned from the results of administering the Probe:

- Use representations and concrete models such as number lines and base-ten blocks to help students' understand division as how many ___ in ___?
- Provide a problem context from which students can make sense of the results.

- Focus on the meaning of the operation before introducing steps of an algorithm.
- Continue to require students to reason about the size of the numbers and the effect of the operation to determine an estimate as a method of checking for the reasonableness of the results of applying an algorithm.

Sample Student Responses to Estimating Quotients

Responses That Suggest Understanding

Sample Student Response 1

Probe Item 1. b. If you have 20 and you want to know how many .5's go into 20, it will double it. Takes two .5 for every 1. That means it is about 40.

Probe Item 2. a. If you have about .5 and want to know how many 2's go into .5 then it can't even be 1.

Probe Item 3. c. If you have about 8 and divide into really small amounts like pennies then it would be a lot. 4 pennies in $1 is 25. 8 of these would be 200.

Sample Student Response 2

Probe Item 1. b. I rounded .54 to 50 and moved the decimal. $50\overline{)2250}$ with 45 on top. 45 is between 40 and 50.

Responses That Suggest Difficulty

Sample Student Response 3

Probe Item 3. b. I am thinking between 20 and 40 makes sense. $8 \div 4$ is 2 but you are talking about decimals here.

Sample Student Response 4

Probe Item 2. a. 0.683 rounds to 1 and 1.9 rounds to 2. $1 \div 2$ is 2. None of the answers work but since I rounded I will pick "a" since it is closest to 2.

Sample Student Response 5

Probe Item 3. b. Estimate then divide, move the decimals to divide. $4\overline{)80}$ with 20 on top.

Division of Fractions

Determine which expression the model represents.

1.

Choose one.	Explain your reasoning.
a. $3 \div \frac{1}{4}$	
b. $2\frac{3}{4} \div 3$	
c. $1 \div 2\frac{3}{4}$	
d. $2\frac{3}{4} \div 1$	

2.

Choose one.	Explain your reasoning.
a. $3 \div 1\frac{1}{4}$	
b. $1\frac{1}{4} \div 3$	
c. $1\frac{1}{4} \div \frac{1}{2}$	
d. $\frac{1}{2} \div 1\frac{1}{4}$	

Teacher Notes: Division Fractions

Questions to Consider About the Key Mathematical Concepts

When solving problems that model division with fractions, can students relate a given model to the numerical expression it represents? To what extent do they

- make sense of the model in terms of the dividend and the divisor?
- relate the model to a numerical expression?
- describe the relationship between the model and the expression?

Common Core Connection (CCSS.Math.Content.6.NS.A.1)

Grade: Sixth

Domain: The Number System

Cluster:

Apply and extend previous understandings of multiplication and division to divide fractions by fractions.

1. Interpret and compute quotients of fractions, and solve word problems involving division of fractions by fractions, e.g., by using visual fraction models and equations to represent the problem.

Uncovering Student Understanding About the Key Concepts

Using the Division of Fractions Probe can provide the following information about how the students are thinking about modeling the division of fractions.

Do they
- correctly interpret the number line representation to determine the size of the dividend and the size of the divisor?

OR

Do they
- correctly determine sizes but reverse the dividend and divisor?

Do they		*Do they*
• determine the size of the divisor?	OR	• focus on the number of equal segments shown?
• describe their choice by relating parts of the model to OR the parts of the expression?		• leave out information about certain parts of the model and/or expression?

Exploring Excerpts From Educational Resources and Related Research

Common areas of difficulty for students:

The common approach of modeling division by drawing pictures of the item and then dividing the item into parts to determine how many parts does not always help students recognize the connection between the model and the numerical expression. Students will need support in making the connection. (Van de Walle, Karp, & Bay-Williams, 2013, p. 331)

"Students often misapply the invert-and-multiply procedure for dividing by a fraction because they lack conceptual understanding of the procedure" (Siegler et al., 2010, p. 29). It is recommended that teachers can use representations such as ribbons or a number line to help students model the division process for fractions in order to build this conceptual understanding of dividing with and by fractions (Siegler et al., p. 33).

Surveying the Prompts and Selected Responses in the Probe

The Probe consists of two separate selected response items. The prompts and selected responses are designed to elicit understandings and common difficulties as described below:

If a student chooses	*It is likely that the student*
1d and 2c (correct answers)	• is able to interpret the number line representation to determine the size of the dividend and the size of the divisor [See Sample Student Response 1]. *Look for indication of the student's understanding in the written explanations of how the student got the answer.*
1c and 2d	• is reversing the dividend and the divisor [See Sample Student Response 2].

(Continued)

(Continued)

If a student chooses	It is likely that the student
1b and 2b	• is able to interpret the number line representation to determine the size of the dividend but counts the number of the divisors as the divisor [See Sample Student Response 3].
1a and 2a	• is reversing the dividend and the divisor as well as counting the number of the divisors as the divisor [See Sample Student Response 4].

Teaching Implications and Considerations

Ideas for eliciting more information from students about their understanding and difficulties:

- Which number in these expressions is considered the dividend? How is the dividend represented in this model?
- Which number in these expressions is considered the divisor? How is the divisor represented in this model?
- How can thinking about division as "how many ___ in ___?" help you determine the correct expression?

Ideas for planning instruction in response to what you learned from the results of administering the Probe:

- Provide multiple opportunities for students to develop models themselves.
- Begin with asking students to model problems within a context.
- When creating models or interpreting models, help students focus on the relationship between the model and the numerical expression representing the operation shown in the model.
- Use number lines as well as models such as area models to help students conceptualize the meaning of dividing by a fraction.

Sample Student Responses to Division Fractions

Responses That Suggest Understanding

Sample Student Response 1

Probe Item 1. d. We learned that division means how many of one size goes into a total size like how many small strips of ribbon can you make from this bigger strip of ribbon. In this one the total size is the solid line which goes from 0 to 2 and $\frac{3}{4}$. The other size is 1 whole. How many 1's go into 2 and $\frac{3}{4}$ is the same as 2 and $\frac{3}{4} \div 1$.

Responses That Suggest Difficulty

Sample Student Response 2

Probe Item 1. c. If you look at the line, there are two things. 2.75 and then three 1's so I think it is $1 \div 2\frac{3}{4}$.

Sample Student Response 3

Probe Item 2. b. Because the line is 1 and then 2 of the 8 which is another $\frac{1}{4}$. And you are dividing by three of the $\frac{1}{2}$'s but the $\frac{1}{2}$'s don't matter so it is $1\frac{1}{4} \div 3$.

Sample Student Response 4

Probe Item 1. a. There are 3 wholes and each whole is split up into 4 sections. So it must be 3 divided by $\frac{1}{4}$.

Number Lines

2.3

For each number line, decide which point reresents the location of the fraction.

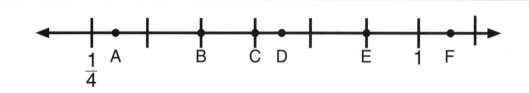

1. $\frac{1}{2}$ Circle One: A   B   C   D   E   F   Not Shown

Explain your choice:

2. $\frac{7}{6}$ Circle One: A   B   C   D   E   F   Not Shown

Explain your choice:

3. $\frac{11}{16}$ Circle One: A   B   C   D   E   F   Not Shown

Explain your choice:

Teacher Notes: Number Lines

Questions to Consider About the
Key Mathematical Concepts

When locating a fraction on the number line, can students determine the whole and the size of the intervals to correctly name a point? To what extent do they

- make sense of the labeled hash marks to determine the whole?
- make sense of the size of the intervals given the whole?
- describe how the whole and the size of the intervals is used to determine the fractions that are represented by the points on the number line?

Common Core Connection
(CCSS.Math.Content.6.NS.C.6)

Grade: Sixth

Domain: The Number System

Cluster:

Apply and extend previous understandings of numbers to the system of rational numbers.

6. Understand a rational number as a point on the number line. Extend number line diagrams and coordinate axes familiar from previous grades to represent points on the line and in the plane with negative number coordinates.

   c. Find and position integers and other rational numbers on a horizontal or vertical number line diagram; find and position pairs of integers and other rational numbers on a coordinate plane.

Uncovering Student Understanding
About the Key Concepts

Using the Number Lines Probe can provide the following information about how the students are thinking about the representations of fractions as points on a number line.

Do they		*Do they*
• correctly determine the whole?	OR	• consider the whole based on the first hash mark to the last hash mark regardless of the labeling?
• correctly determine the size of the intervals?	OR	• simply count the hash marks regardless of whether they are equally spaced; or • rely only on benchmarking or estimating rather than on finding the actual size?
• describe how they used information about the whole and the size of the intervals to name the point representing the given fraction?	OR	• describe counting or estimating with benchmarks?

Exploring Excerpts From Educational Resources and Related Research

Common areas of difficulty for students:

Many middle school students are still unable to locate a simple fraction to a right place on a number line. "Their problem seems mainly to be in being unable to identify the whole correctly as well as sticking to a part-whole schema." (Hannula, 2003, p. 34)

Number line tasks pose challenges for students and often tasks used in classroom instruction, which are often between 0 and 1 with equally portioned intervals, may inadvertently mask students' understanding. . . . By providing number lines with unequal partitions and/or non-zero to 1 labels, it can be determined whether students' are considering distances on the number line or merely counting parts regardless of length. (Shaughnessy, 2011, pp. 431–432)

Surveying the Prompts and Selected Responses in the Probe

The Probe consists of three related multiple selection response items. The prompts and selected responses are designed to elicit understandings and common difficulties as described in the following table:

If a student chooses	It is likely that the student
1B, 2 Not Shown, 3D (correct answers)	• is able to interpret the number line representation to determine the size of the whole, the size of the intervals, and the fraction that names the point [See Sample Student Response 1]. *Look for indication of the student's understanding in the written explanations of how the student got the answer.*
1C or 1D	• is finding the halfway point of the line rather than the point $\frac{1}{2}$ [See Sample Student Responses 2 and 3].
2F	• is using an estimate rather than an exact location [See Sample Student Response 4].
3 Not Shown	• doesn't see how the number line can be divided into 16ths [See Sample Student Response 5]; and/or • has difficulty determining numbers in between given hash marks [See Sample Student Response 6].
Misc. other answers	• is counting on or counting all in a variety of ways and using those incorrect counts to determine the name of the point [See Sample Student Response 7]; and/or • using benchmarks incorrectly [See Sample Student Response 8].

Teaching Implications and Considerations

Ideas for eliciting more information from students about their understanding and difficulties:

- Does the number line show the whole? Can you explain what the whole is?
- What are you referring to as the intervals? Show me.
- How might you find the exact location rather than an estimate?

Ideas for planning instruction in response to what you learned from the results of administering the Probe:

- Use a variety of number lines with different parts of the whole shown as well as more than one whole shown.
- Ask students to name given points as well as to place points when given a fraction and a number line.
- Have students build their own number lines with various start and end points and different-sized intervals.

- Estimating and finding actual answers are both instructionally important. Work with students to establish when an estimate versus an actual answer is appropriate.

Sample Student Responses to Number Lines

Responses That Suggest Understanding

Sample Student Response 1

Probe Item 1. B. Label every other mark by 4ths. B is $\frac{2}{4}$ which is same as $\frac{1}{2}$.

Probe Item 2. Not Shown. Label each mark by 8ths. In between would have to be 16ths, not 6ths. F is close but not right.

Probe Item 3. D. Like I said. In between is 16ths. Count out the in betweens to get to 11 and it's gotta be D.

Responses That Suggest Difficulty

Sample Student Response 2

Probe Item 1. C. It is about in the middle off all the other tick marks.

Sample Student Response 3

Probe Item 1. D. I 'liminated one hash mark from each end until there was one left. What was left was D.

Sample Student Response 4

Probe Item 2. F. It is the only one more than 1.

Sample Student Response 5

Probe Item 3. Not Shown. The little lines have to be 8ths. So $\frac{11}{16}$ is not there.

Sample Student Response 6

Probe Item 3. Not Shown I put the numbers under the lines but don't know what is between them. Maybe like $2\frac{5}{4}$ or something like that but don't know.

Sample Student Response 7

Probe Item 2. Not Shown. If you count the lines and dots, you don't have 6 of 'em, there are 11. So there is no $\frac{7}{6}$.

Sample Student Response 8

Probe Item 3. E. I know $\frac{11}{16}$ is about $\frac{3}{4}$ and E is about $\frac{3}{4}$ of the way to 1.

Rational Number Multiplication Estimates

Estimate the product without calculating. Circle the best estimate.	Explain your thinking.
1. $$\left(-1\frac{2}{3}\right)\left(2\frac{1}{2}\right)$$ a. −4 d. 2 b. −2 e. 4 c. 1 f. 6	
2. $$\left(\frac{6}{7}\right)\left(-\frac{4}{5}\right)$$ a. −2 d. $\frac{1}{2}$ b. −1 e. 1 c. $-\frac{1}{2}$ f. 2	
3. $$\left(-4\frac{1}{3}\right)\left(-\frac{3}{5}\right)$$ a. −4 d. $\frac{1}{2}$ b. −2 e. 2 c. $-\frac{1}{2}$ f. 4	

Source: Adapted from Rose Tobey and Minton (2011).

Teacher Notes: Rational Number Multiplication Estimates

Questions to Consider About the Key Mathematical Concepts

When estimating the products of rational numbers, can students reason about the size and sign of the numbers and the effect of the operation? To what extent do they

- make sense of size of the numbers involved?
- make sense of the effect of multiplying with positive and negative numbers?
- describe how to use this reasoning to determine a reasonable estimate?

Common Core Connection (CCSS.Math.Content.7.NS.A.2)

Grade: Seventh

Domain: The Number System

Cluster:

Apply and extend previous understandings of operations with fractions to add, subtract, multiply, and divide rational numbers.

2. Apply and extend previous understandings of multiplication and division and of fractions to multiply and divide rational numbers.

Uncovering Student Understanding About the Key Concepts

Using the Rational Number Multiplication Estimates Probe can provide the following information about how the students are thinking about estimating the products of rational numbers:

Do they		*Do they*
• reason correctly about the size of the numbers?	OR	• apply incorrect benchmarking strategies?
• reason correctly about the size of the product?	OR	• apply an overgeneralization of "multiplication always results in a bigger answer"?
• apply the correct rules for multiplying signed numbers?	OR	• overgeneralize from rules for combining signed numbers

*E*xploring Excerpts From Educational Resources and Related Research

Common areas of difficulty for students:

Multiplying and dividing fractions and decimals can be challenging for many students because of problems that are primarily conceptual rather than procedural. From their experience with whole numbers, many students appear to develop a belief that "multiplication makes bigger and division makes smaller." (NCTM, 2000, p. 218)

Errors show that many students have learned rules for manipulating symbols without understanding what those symbols mean or why the rules work. Many students are unable to reason appropriately about symbols for rational numbers and do not have the strategic competence that would allow them to catch their mistakes. (NRC, 2001, p. 234)

Developing fluency requires a balance and connection between conceptual understanding and computational proficiency. Computational methods that are overpracticed without understanding are often forgotten or remembered incorrectly (Hiebert 1999; Kamii, Lewis, and Livingston 1993; Hiebert and Lindquist 1990). (NCTM, 2000, p. 35)

*S*urveying the Prompts and Selected Responses in the Probe

The Probe consists of three separate selected response items. The prompts and selected responses are designed to elicit understandings and common difficulties as described below:

If a student chooses	*It is likely that the student*
1a, 2b, 3e (correct answers)	• is correctly reasoning about the size and sign of the numbers and the effect of the operation [See Sample Student Response 1]; or • has correctly applied an algorithm rather than using reasoning to determine an estimate [See Sample Student Response 2]. *Look for indication of the student's understanding in the written explanations of how the student got the answer.*

(Continued)

(Continued)

If a student chooses	It is likely that the student
1e, 2e, 3b	• has overgeneralized rules from adding integers: take the sign of the larger number and negative plus a negative is a negative [See Sample Student Response 3].
1e, 2e or 2f, 3f	• is applying the incorrect rule of "multiplication makes bigger" [See Sample Student Response 4].
Various other patterns	• inconsistently applies correct reasoning about either the size of the fraction or the effect of the operation [See Sample Student Response 5]; or • has incorrectly applied an algorithm [See Sample Student Response 6].

Variation Rational Number Estimates: Quotients

Teaching Implications and Considerations

Ideas for eliciting more information from students about their understanding and difficulties:

- For students who incorrectly reason about the size of the numbers, ask, "Without thinking about the sign, what benchmark or whole number is this number close to?"
- For students who apply the "multiplication makes bigger" rule, ask, "How can you model $\frac{1}{2} \times \frac{3}{4}$?" If they are able to correctly show half of three-fourths, ask, "Is this answer bigger than $\frac{1}{2}$?"
- For students who apply an algorithm rather than estimating, ask, "How might you think about this without actually calculating an answer?"

Ideas for planning instruction in response to what you learned from the results of administering the Probe:

- Use representations and concrete models such as number lines and area models to help students understand multiplication as __ of __.
- Provide multiple examples of products that are larger than the factor as well as smaller than the factor so that students can generalize about the size of the product without calculating or modeling the problem.
- Focus on the meaning of the operation before introducing steps of an algorithm.

- Continue to require students to reason about the size of the numbers and the effect of the operation to determine an estimate as a method of checking for the reasonableness of the results of applying an algorithm.

Sample Student Responses to Rational Number Multiplication Estimates

Responses That Suggest Understanding

Sample Student Response 1

Probe Item 1. a. I know neg times pos is neg. I also know 2 × 2.5 is about 5 so the closest number is −4.

Probe Item 2. b. I know pos times neg is neg and 1 × 1 is 1 so −1 is closest to the real answer.

Probe Item 3. e. This time neg times neg is pos. $4 \times \frac{1}{2}$ is 2.

Sample Student Response 2

Probe Item 1. a. $-\frac{5}{3} \times \frac{5}{2} = -\frac{25}{6} = -\frac{25}{6}$. This is $-4\frac{1}{6}$ which rounds to −4.

Responses That Suggest Difficulty

Sample Student Response 3

Probe Item 1. e. Sign depends on biggest one so positive because $2\frac{1}{2}$ is bigger of them. Almost 2 times $2\frac{1}{2}$ will be about 4 like e.

Sample Student Response 4

Probe Item 2. a. Like number 1, I circled the biggest number with the correct sign. This one has to be (−) so −2 is my answer.

Sample Student Response 5

Probe Item 3. f. Round each number. −4 × −1 is +4.

Sample Student Response 6

Probe Item 3. f. $-4 \times -\frac{1}{3} = -4$ and $\frac{1}{3} \times \frac{3}{5}$. $\frac{1}{3} \times \frac{3}{5}$ is $\frac{1}{5}$ so the answer is about $4\frac{1}{5}$ which is f.

Variation: Rational Number Division Estimates

Estimate without calculating. Circle the best estimate.	Explain your thinking.
1. $$-2\frac{2}{5} \div \frac{1}{2}$$ a. −4 d. $\frac{1}{2}$ b. −1 e. 1 c. $-\frac{1}{2}$ f. 4	
2. $$-3\frac{6}{7} \div \frac{7}{8}$$ a. −6 d. 2 b. −4 e. 4 c. −2 f. 6	
3. $$-\frac{5}{9} \div 1\frac{1}{8}$$ a. −2 d. $\frac{1}{2}$ b. −1 e. 1 c. $-\frac{1}{2}$ f. 2	

Source: Adapted from Rose Tobey and Minton (2011).

HPB-Ohio
3860 La Reunion Pkwy.
Dallas, TX 75212
serviceohio@hpb.com

Items:

Qty Title   Locator

1 Uncovering Student Thinking Abou... L01-2-17-014-001-51

Marketplace: Abebooks
Order Number: 4290715
Ship Method: Standard
Customer Name: Thomas Wagner
Order Date: 2/2/2020 12:00:00 AM
Marketplace Order #: 548821457
Email: thomas.w.wagner@gmail.com

2.5

Is It Positive?

Without actually calculating, use reasoning to determine whether the expression results in a POSITIVE answer.

Circle Yes or No.	Explain your choice.
a. −(−53.4 + 92.3) Yes No	
b. −34.23 − 27.9 Yes No	
c. $\dfrac{-5.3 - 3.6}{(-3.2)(-4.3)}$ Yes No	
d. −2.4 − (−3.4 • −6.4) Yes No	

Teacher Notes: Is It Positive?

Questions to Consider About the Key Mathematical Concepts

When solving problems involving operating with positive and negative numbers, can students reason about the size of the numbers and the effect of the operation? To what extent do they

- make sense of the size of positive and negative numbers?
- make sense of the effect of the operations involved?
- describe their reasoning about estimating with positive and negative numbers?

**Common Core Connection
(CCSS.Math.Content.7.NS.A.1; CCSS.Math.
Content.7.NS.A.2)**

Grade: Seventh

Domain: The Number System

Cluster:

Apply and extend previous understandings of operations with fractions.

1. Apply and extend previous understandings of addition and subtraction to add and subtract rational numbers.

2. Apply and extend previous understandings of multiplication and division and of fractions to multiply and divide rational numbers.

Uncovering Student Understanding About the Key Concepts

Using the Is It Positive? Probe can provide the following information about how the students are thinking about operations with positive and negative numbers.

Do they

- correctly apply rules or shortcuts learned about positive and negative numbers?

OR

Do they

- overgeneralize procedural shortcuts (rules) such as two negatives "always" make a positive?

Do they

- reason about the given numbers   OR
  and operations involved
  without actually calculating an
  answer?

Do they

- rely on actual calculations to
  obtain an answer?

Variation: Are You Positive? Examples and Nonexamples

Exploring Excerpts From Educational Resources and Related Research

Common areas of difficulty for students:

Developing fluency requires a balance and connections between conceptual understanding and computational proficiency. Computational methods that are overpracticed without understanding are often forgotten or remembered incorrectly (Hiebert 1999; Kamii, Lewis, and Livingston 1993; Hiebert and Lindquist 1990). (NCTM, 2000, p. 35)

Students misapply rules they have learned as isolated, mathematical procedures. The learning of facts and algorithms needs to be a building stone of the active mathematical knowledge of students. (NCTM, 2003, p. 114)

"Research in cognition suggests that it is critical for students to play around with ideas before formal versions are introduced. When formalization is introduced too early, it interferes with the development of students' conceptual understanding (Pesek & Kirshner, 2000)." (Choppin et al., 2012, p. 554)

The addition and subtraction of integers is one of the first major avenues, and roadblocks, to student success in the learning of algebra. Unfortunately, many students cannot make, or have a very difficult time making, the transition from working with whole numbers to working with integers. Students who struggle and do not succeed in making this transition undoubtedly find themselves at a disadvantage when trying to make sense of subsequent mathematical concepts that rely on their proficiency with and understanding of the addition, subtraction, multiplication, and division of integers. (Ponce, 2007, p. 10)

Surveying the Prompts and Selected Responses in the Probe

The Probe consists of four separate selected response items. The prompts and selected responses are designed to elicit understandings and common difficulties as described in the following table:

If a student chooses	It is likely that the student
No for all responses (correct answer)	• has an accurate conceptual understanding of integers and/ or is proficient in computational strategies with them. This is not necessarily true for those who used a calculator to obtain an answer [See Sample Student Response 1]. *Look for indication of the student's understanding in the written explanations of how the student got the answer.*
Yes for all responses	• does not have a conceptual or procedural understanding of computations with integers. Students often inaccurately remember or misuse shortcut rules that they have been taught [See Sample Student Responses 2–5].

Teaching Implications and Considerations

Ideas for eliciting more information from students about their understanding and difficulties:

- For students who apply an incorrect rule, provide a simpler problem and ask, "Can you write a contextual problem to represent the expressions shown?"
- For students who apply an algorithm rather than estimating, ask, "How might you think about this without actually calculating an answer?"

Ideas for planning instruction in response to what you learned from the results of administering the Probe:

- There should be a balance between conceptual understanding and computational fluency.
- Provide opportunities for students to work with integers within a context. "Canceling debt provides a natural interpretation of taking away a negative amount" (Tillema, 2012, p. 474). "[Ask] students to consider that if 3×-4 is 'adding three $4 debits' (adding -12), then could -3×-4 be interpreted as 'removing three $4 debits' (taking away -12), which results in an increase of $12 to net profit." (Gregg & Gregg, 2007, p. 50)
- Students should spend time exploring positive and negative numbers and operations on them in a variety of contexts and with manipulatives, number lines, technology, etc.
- Students should be given ample time and opportunities to reason about numbers and computations with them. It is important for this to take place before they are formalized and procedural shortcuts are learned.

Sample Student Responses to Is It Positive?

Responses That Suggest Understanding

Sample Student Response 1

Probe Item A. No. Inside ( ) is + so −(+) is negative no matter what.

Probe Item B. No. Subtracting a − from a − is always more into the negative numbers.

Probe Item C. No. Top has to be −, bottom has to be +. Now (−) ÷ (+) is always negative.

Probe Item D. No. Inside ( ) is +. This is now same as B above. So it is negative.

Responses That Suggest Difficulty

Sample Student Response 2

Probe Item B. Yes. Because (−) − will change to positive.

Sample Student Response 3

Probe Item D. Yes. −2.4 − (+big number). Since big number is +, answer is positive.

Sample Student Response 4

Probe Item A. Yes. Two negative signs right together.

Sample Student Response 5

Probe Item C. Yes. Two in numerator and two in denominator. All will cancel.

Variation: Are You Positive?

2.5V

Without calculating the actual answer: Circle all problems that result in a POSITIVE answer.

a. $-(53 + 92)$ b. $-34 - 27$ c. $93 - (-56)$

d. $(-24)(35)$ e. $(-34)(-54)$ f. $-34 + 56$

g. $\dfrac{-5}{-2}$ h. $\dfrac{-5-10}{-(-2)}$

Describe the process that you used to decide whether the problem resulted in a positive answer:

Number Card Sort

2.6

Reproducible student cards and Recording Sheet follow Teacher Notes on p. 60

Rational	Irrational
a. $\sqrt{2}$	b. $\sqrt{25}$
c. $\dfrac{1}{3}$	d. Π
e. $\dfrac{5}{0}$	f. $\sqrt{3} \cdot \sqrt{3}$
g. $\sqrt{2} \cdot \sqrt{5}$	h. $\dfrac{10}{9}$

i. $-\sqrt{9}$	j. $\dfrac{22}{7}$
k. $\dfrac{5.3}{7.2}$	l. $(\sqrt{3})(-\sqrt{3})$
m. $\dfrac{0}{4}$	n. $0.8\overline{3}$
o. $\dfrac{\sqrt{5}}{\sqrt{3}}$	p. $\dfrac{-8}{\sqrt{7}}$

Advance Preparation: Create cards by photocopying on card stock and cutting. Separate the two blank cards and the two label cards from the deck and shuffle the rest of the cards.

Instructions:

1. Invite the student(s) to sort the cards into two piles: **Rational** and **Irrational**. Use the label cards to identify the piles.

2. As students finish the sort, give them the blank cards and ask them to create their own **Rational** and **Irrational** examples (two of each).

3. Either choose three cards for the student or ask the student to choose three cards from the **Rational** pile. Ask him to explain how he knew these cards should go in the **Rational** pile.

4. Either choose three cards for the student or ask the student to choose three cards from the **Irrational** pile. Ask her to explain how she knew these cards should go in the **Irrational** pile. Use the recording sheet as appropriate.

Teacher Notes: Number Card Sort

Questions to Consider About the Key Mathematical Concepts

When classifying numbers, can students determine whether a number is rational or irrational or whether the result of computing two numbers will result in a rational or irrational number? To what extent do they

- base their classification on the characteristics of rational and irrational numbers?
- understand the effect of the operation of two irrational numbers and/or a rational number and an irrational number?

Common Core Connection (CCSS.Math.Content.8.NS.A.1)

Grade: Eighth

Domain: The Number System

Cluster:

Know that there are numbers that are not rational, and approximate them by rational numbers.

1. Know that numbers that are not rational are called irrational. Understand informally that every number has a decimal expansion; for rational numbers, show that the decimal expansion repeats eventually, and convert a decimal expansion which repeats eventually into a rational number.

Uncovering Student Understanding About the Key Concepts

Using the Number Card Sort Probe can provide the following information about how the students are thinking about the characteristics of rational and irrational numbers.

Do they

- understand that irrational numbers can't be turned into fractions, and are nonrepeating and nonterminating?

OR

Do they

- think any number that "goes on forever" is an irrational number?
- assume a square root is always irrational?

Do they

- Understand that the ratio of two rational numbers is always rational and the ratio of a rational and an irrational is always irrational?

OR

Do they

- consider some ratios of rational number to rational number as irrational; or

- consider some ratios of irrational number to irrational number as rational?

Variation: Is it Irrational? Selected Response

Exploring Excerpts From Educational Resources and Related Research

Common areas of difficulty for students:

There are numerous pieces of research that confirm several cognition problems about the real numbers (Zazkis and Sirotic, 2004; Moseley, 2005). Particularly, many studies show that students face difficulties in identifying rational and irrational numbers. The distinction between the different categories of numbers remains fuzzy and strongly dependent on their semiotic representations (O'Connor, 2001; Munyazikwiye, 1995). (Giannakoulias, Souyoul, & Zachariades, 2007, p. 416)

Many students seem to equate π with $\frac{22}{7}$ and 3.14. In other words they treat all the three to be equivalent. Many students had equated π as 3.14 and concluded it to be rational. This could be attributed to the erroneous practice of substituting π as 3.14 in computations involving areas and volumes of solid figures. Those students who had concluded $\frac{22}{7}$ to be irrational knew π to be irrational but failed to appreciate the difference between its actual value and approximate representation. This can also be due to the practice of approximate arithmetic, which they are used to, both inside and outside the classroom. (Parameswaran, n.d., p. 168)

Surveying the Prompts and Selected Responses in the Probe

The Probe consists of multiple examples of rational and irrational numbers as well as numerical expressions involving rational and irrational numbers. The prompts and selected responses are designed to elicit understandings and common difficulties as described in the following table:

If a student chooses	It is likely that the student
Irrational: a, d, g, o, p Rational: b, c, e, f, h, i, j, k, l, m, n (correct categorization)	• is basing his classification on the characteristics of rational and irrational numbers [See Sample Student Response 1]. *Look for indication of the student's understanding in the written explanations of how the student got the answer.*
Irrational: c, e, h, n	• views nonterminating decimals as irrational numbers [See Sample Student Response 2].
Irrational: m	• is confusing the number with dividing by 0, which is undefined and not rational [See Sample Student Response 3].
Irrational: e, k	• believes that you can't have decimals within fractions and confuses this with the meaning of irrational [See Sample Student Response 4].
Irrational: j	• believes $\frac{22}{7}$ is equivalent to π [See Sample Student Response 5].

Teaching Implications and Considerations

Ideas for eliciting more information from students about their understanding and difficulties:

- How would you describe the characteristics of an irrational number? Does this particular number have those characteristics?
- How would you describe the characteristics of a rational number? Does this particular number have those characteristics?
- Why do we sometimes substitute 3.14 for π?
- What does it mean to take the square root of a number? How can that help you determine whether the numbers are irrational or rational?

Ideas for planning instruction in response to what you learned from the results of administering the Probe:

- Explore irrational numbers through square roots of whole numbers. Support students' understanding by making explicit when approximate versus actual values are in play.
- Establish that irrational numbers are real numbers whose locations can be approximated on the number line.

- Connect these ideas when using the Pythagorean Theorem to find lengths of sides of right triangles.
- Help students generalize ideas related to real numbers by asking them to justify when statements about rational and irrational numbers are sometimes, always, or never true, such as those from Shell Center Team (located at map.mathshell.org/materials/download.php? fileid=1245 and map.mathshell.org/materials/download.php?fileid=1267).

Sample Student Responses to Number Card Sort

Responses That Suggest Understanding

Sample Student Response 1

I just knew what to look for. Irrational has to be nonstopping and has no pattern of repeating numbers in the decimal part. I changed anything that wasn't a decimal into a decimal to check to be sure.

Responses That Suggest Difficulty

Sample Student Response 2

Anything that doesn't end is irrational.

Sample Student Response 3

If it goes on and on (you have to pretend if using a calculator) or doesn't work like the 0 card (I got an E for this on my calculator).

Sample Student Response 4

Irrational is nonrepeating and nonterminating decimal numbers and any fraction that isn't just numbers in the top and bottom. Things like $\frac{2.4}{5}$ and $\frac{\sqrt{2}}{3}$ are good fractions.

Sample Student Response 5

Well, you said it is like pi and pi is irrational.

Number Card Sort

Rational	Irrational
a. $\sqrt{2}$	b. $\sqrt{25}$
c. $\dfrac{1}{3}$	d. Π
e. $\dfrac{5}{0}$	f. $\sqrt{3} \cdot \sqrt{3}$
g) $\sqrt{2} \cdot \sqrt{5}$	h) $\dfrac{10}{9}$

i. $-\sqrt{9}$	j. $\dfrac{22}{7}$
k. $\dfrac{5.3}{7.2}$	l. $(\sqrt{3})(-\sqrt{2})$
m. $\dfrac{0}{4}$	n. $0.8\bar{3}$
o. $\dfrac{\sqrt{5}}{\sqrt{3}}$	p. $\dfrac{-8}{\sqrt{7}}$

Recording Sheet: Number Sort

Proportional Cards	Explanation

Not Proportional Cards	Explanation

Variation: Is It Irrational?

Students were asked to come up with examples of Irrational Numbers. Four students gave the following examples:

Student	Circle One	Explain your choice.
Samantha	Agree or Disagree	
Felipe	Agree or Disagree	
Elijah	Agree or Disagree	
Kayla	Agree or Disagree	

3

Ratio and Proportional Relationship Probes

The content of the Probes in this chapter aligns with the standards for Grades 6 and 7. The Probes and their variations will also be relevant beyond the aligned grade level for students in higher grades who have not yet met standards from previous grade levels, as well as for students who have already met the standards at their own grade level.

We developed these Probes to address this critical area of focus for middle school students, described in the standards (CCSSO, 2010) as follows:

> The content of the Probes in this chapter aligns with the standards for Grades 6 and 7. The Probes and their variations will also be relevant beyond the aligned grade level for students in higher grades who have not yet met standards from previous grade levels, as well as for students who have already met the standards at their own grade level.

- Understand ratio concepts and use ratio reasoning to solve problems.
- Analyze proportional relationships and use them to solve real-world and mathematical problems.

Common Core Math Content

Common Core Mathematical Content	Related Question	Probe Name
Use ratio and rate reasoning to solve real-world and mathematical problems. CCSS.Math.Content.6.RP.A.3	When solving problems involving percents, can students reason about the size of the numbers involved in order to provide a best estimate of the missing value?	Best Estimates: Finding Percents (p. 66) Variation: Finding the Percent of a Number (p. 70)
Use ratio reasoning to convert measurement units. CCSS.Math.Content.6.RP.A.3d	Do students apply ratio reasoning about the relationship between the sizes of two different units along with reasoning about the inverse relationship between the size of the unit and the number of units needed to measure an object's length?	Comparing Measures (p. 71)
Recognize and represent proportional relationships between quantities. CCSS.Math.Content.7.RP.A.2	When solving proportional reasoning problems, can students use estimation skills to find an equivalent ratio representation?	Best Estimates: Solving Proportions (p. 75)
Recognize and represent proportional relationships between quantities. CCSS.Math.Content.7.RP.A.2	When solving problems involving proportional reasoning, can students distinguish between proportional and nonproportional relationships?	Proportional Reasoning Sort (p. 80) Variation: Is It a Proportional Relationship? (p. 90)

Best Estimates: Finding Percents

Without calculating, determine the best estimate.

Choose the best *estimate.*	Explain your choice.
1. **What is 5.3% of 41.9?** a. 20 b. 8 c. 2	
2. **What % of 5.1 is 15.6?** a. 300 b. 30 c. 3	
3. **0.3% of what is 19.8?** a. 6,000 b. 600 c. 60	

Teacher Notes: Best Estimates: Finding Percents

Questions to Consider About the Key Mathematical Concepts

When solving problems involving percents, can students reason about the size of the numbers involved in order to provide a best estimate of the missing value? To what extent do they

- make sense of percent as a rate per 100?
- determine the relationship between the percent and the numbers?
- correctly reason about an estimate given any missing amount (e.g., finding the whole, given the part and the percent)?

Common Core Connection (CCSS.Math.Content.6.RP.A.3c)

Grade: Sixth

Domain: Ratios and Proportional Relationships

Cluster:

Understand ratio concepts and use ratio reasoning to solve problems.

3c. Find a percent of a quantity as a rate per 100 (e.g., 30% of a quantity means $\frac{30}{100}$ times the quantity); solve problems involving finding the whole, given a part and the percent.

Uncovering Student Understanding About the Key Concepts

Using the Best Estimates: Finding Percents Probe can provide the following information about how the students are thinking about the relationships between the whole, the given part, and the percent.

Do they		*Do they*
• reason correctly about the percent involved?	OR	• apply incorrect reasoning such as 5.3% is about 0.5 or half of?
• reason correctly to determine the missing amount?	OR	• revert to using an algorithm (incorrectly or correctly) to solve the problem?

Exploring Excerpts From Educational Resources and Related Research

Common areas of difficulty for students:

Students may view percents simply as an alternative way of writing decimals or fractions rather than as special representations of relationships between two quantities. Overemphasis on equality between fraction, decimal, and percent forms masks the many meanings and uses of percents. (Bay Area Mathematics Task Force, 1999, p. 92)

"The central challenge of developing students' capacity to think with ratios (to reason proportionally) is to teach ideas and restrain the quick path to computation" (Smith 2002, p. 15). A possible reason for why students may not apply cross-multiplication even when taught is that the method does not connect with conceptual approaches. (Van de Walle et al., 2013, p. 371)

Data from the Mathematics Assessment for Learning and Teaching (MaLT) project data base indicate that students demonstrate the following types of difficulties with percent problems: the % sign prompts a division error . . . , dividing larger number by smaller number regardless of relationship, and errors in determining percent to decimal equivalence. (Ryan & Williams, 2007, pp. 174, 207–208)

Surveying the Prompts and Selected Responses in the Probe

The Probe consists of three separate selected response items. The prompts and selected responses are designed to elicit understandings and common difficulties as described below:

If a student chooses	*It is likely that the student*
1c, 2a, 3a (correct answers)	• is applying correct reasoning about the relationship between the percent, the part, and the whole [See Sample Student Response 1]. • is correctly using an algorithm without estimating [See Sample Student Response 2]. *Look for indication of the student's understanding in the written explanations of how the student got the answer.*
Various other answer patterns	• is dividing the larger number by the smaller number without reasoning about the size of the percent or the relationship between the percent, the part, and the whole [See Sample Student Responses 3–5].

Teaching Implications and Considerations

Ideas for eliciting more information from students about their understanding and difficulties:

- What is an approximate decimal equivalent to the percent given in the problem?
- Which number represents the whole? the part?
- What is true about the percent if the part is larger than the whole?

Ideas for planning instruction in response to what you learned from the results of administering the Probe:

- Build students' conceptual understanding of percent as a rate per 100 by using models such as the 10 × 10 grid.
- Provide multiple types of percent problems where students can relate the part and the whole to a given context.
- Use representations such as ratio tables and double number lines to help students find equivalent ratios and determine missing quantities.
- Delay use of proportions and cross-multiplication until students have an understanding of concepts related to finding percents. Connect the steps of the procedure to the former more intuitive approaches.

Sample Student Responses to Best Estimates: Finding Percents

Responses That Suggest Understanding

Sample Student Response 1

Probe Item 1. c. 5.3% is about $\frac{1}{20}$. 40 divided by 20 is 2.

Probe Item 2. a. 15.6 is more than 5. The only way that happens is if there is more than 100%.

Probe Item 3. a. 0.3 percent is a really small amount so the number would have to be really really big. 1% of 600 is 6 so 0.3 would be even smaller so it has to be 6,000.

Sample Student Response 2

Probe Item 2. a. I set up the equation $x * 5.1 = 15.6$ the divided. [Shows division problem with 3.058 . . . as the answer.]

Responses That Suggest Difficulty

Sample Student Response 3:

Probe Item 1. b. 40 divided by 5 is 8.

Sample Student Response 4:

Probe Item 3. c. 18 divided by 3 is 6 but it's a 0.3 so 60.

Variation: Finding the Percent of a Number

The following students used mental math to estimate **5.3%** of **41.9**.

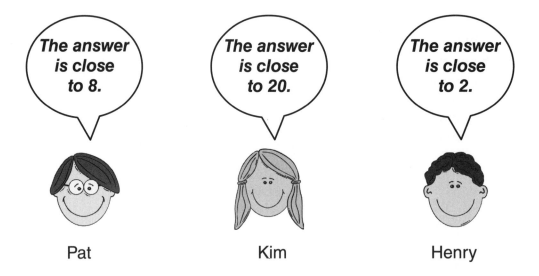

Pat   Kim   Henry

Circle the name of the student you agree with: Pat   Kim   Henry

Justify your choice:

Comparing Measures

Two students were asked to measure the length of a desk using an eraser, a pencil, a thumbtack, or a paperclip. The picture shows how these Items compare in size.

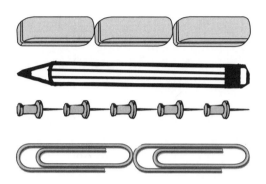

Kyra and Toby both measured the same desk using one of the items from the picture above.

Kyra: I got 12!

Toby: I got 8!

If both of them measured correctly, what item did each measure with?

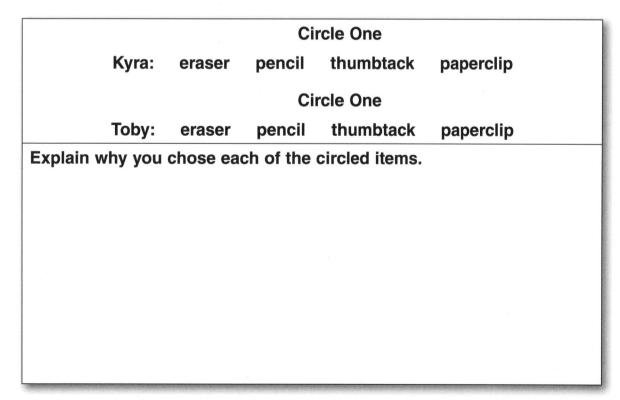

Circle One			
Kyra: eraser	pencil	thumbtack	paperclip

Circle One			
Toby: eraser	pencil	thumbtack	paperclip

Explain why you chose each of the circled items.

Teacher Notes: Comparing Measures

Questions to Consider About the Key Mathematical Concepts

Do students apply ratio reasoning about the relationship between the sizes of two different units along with reasoning about the inverse relationship between the size of the unit and the number of units needed to measure an object's length? To what extent do they

- apply correct reasoning about the ratio of the lengths of two different objects?
- understand that to span an object's length, smaller same-size units require more iterations than larger same-size units?

Common Core Connection (CCSS.Math.Content.6.RP.A.3d)

Grade: Sixth

Domain: Ratios and Proportional Relationships

Cluster:

Understand ratio concepts and use ratio reasoning to solve problems.

3d. Use ratio reasoning to convert measurement units; manipulate and transform units appropriately when multiplying or dividing quantities.

Uncovering Student Understanding About the Key Concepts

Using the Comparing Measures Probe can provide the following information about how the students are thinking about measurement.

Do they

- know that the smaller the unit the more iterations (larger number of units in the measure)/the larger the unit the fewer iterations (smaller number of units in the measure)?

OR

- look at the relationship between the sizes of the units?

OR

Do they

- associate the larger unit with the larger number of units in the measure and/or the smaller unit with the smaller number of units in the measure?

- use other incorrect reasoning, such as additive reasoning, to determine the answer?

Exploring Excerpts From Educational Resources and Related Research

Common areas of difficulty for students:

Concepts of measurement play a large role in understanding rational numbers and multiplicative reasoning. . . . Unfortunately some older students do not fully understand such measurement principles as the compensatory principle: the smaller the unit of measure, the more of those units you will need to measure something. (Lamon, 2006, pp. 40–42)

Students do not always recognize multiplicative situations and instead apply additive reasoning. . . . A variety of contexts and assessment structures are needed to ensure students are able to determine when a situation calls for multiplicative reasoning. (Bright, Joyner, & Wallis, 2003, pp. 166–172)

Surveying the Prompts and Selected Responses in the Probe

The Probe consists of two related selected response items. The prompts and selected responses are designed to elicit understandings and common difficulties as described below:

If a student chooses	It is likely that the student
Kyra – eraser Toby – paperclip (correct choices)	• understands the longer unit will result in a smaller count of the unit in the measure and the 3:2 relationship between the pencil and paperclip [See Sample Student Response 1]. *Look for indication of the student's understanding in the written explanations of how the student got the answer.*
Kyra – paperclip Toby – eraser	• notices the 3:2 relationship between the pencil and paperclip but connects the longer unit to the larger number of units in the length [See Sample Student Response 2].
Kyra – pencil Toby – tacks	• uses additive reasoning when comparing one pencil to five tacks seeing the difference of four [See Sample Student Response 3].
Other various choices	• is not paying attention to the relationship between the measures or is thinking the desks are of different sizes [See Sample Student Response 4].

Teaching Implications and Considerations

Ideas for eliciting more information from students about their understanding and difficulties:

- Be prepared with an eraser, pencil, tack, and paperclip (these do not need to have the same relationship between the sizes as those in the picture). Have the students measure the length of the paper with two of the objects. Ask whether there were more units in the count with the longer object or short object.
- Ask about the relationship between the units. For example, what is the relationship between the number of tacks and the number of paperclips?

Ideas for planning instruction in response to what you learned from the results of administering the Probe:

- When using length measures, make inferences about the sizes of the units as well as the length of the object. Use ratio reasoning to describe the relationship between the sizes of the units.
- Help students generalize the inverse relationship between sizes of units and the number of units needed to measure an object's length by using various nonstandard and standard units.
- Connect this foundational knowledge to more formal procedures for converting between units of measure.

Sample Student Responses to Comparing Measures

Responses That Suggest Understanding

Sample Student Response 1

Kyra, erasers, and Toby, paperclips. 12 to 8 is a 3 to 2 ratio. The eraser and paperclip is 3 to 2. Kyra has to have erasers because she needs more than what Toby has to measure the desk.

Responses That Suggest Difficulty

Sample Student Response 2

Kyra, paperclips, and Toby, eraser. I tried lots of combinations till I figured out the erasers and paperclips both could work. 4 sets of paperclips and 4 sets of erasers. Kyra is using paperclips 'cuz those are bigger.

Sample Student Response 3:

Kyra, tacks, and Toby, pencil. There are 4 more tacks then 1 pencil just like 12 − 4 is 8.

Sample Student Response 3

Circles all choices for both. Really any of them could work because it depends on what you are measuring.

Best Estimates: Solving Proportions

Without calculating, determine the best estimate.

Choose the best estimate for *x*.	Explain your choice.
1. $$\frac{15.2}{4.8} = \frac{x}{7.4}$$ a. 18 b. 21 c. 10	
2. $$\frac{1.2}{x} = \frac{2.5}{8.3}$$ a. 4 b. 2 c. 6	

Teacher Notes: Best Estimates: Solving Proportions

Questions to Consider About the Key Mathematical Concepts

When solving proportional reasoning problems, can students use estimation skills to find an equivalent ratio representation? To what extent do they

- determine and use the multiplicative relationship between two ratios?
- describe how they use estimation and reasoning skills to find an appropriate ratio to make an equivalent proportion?

Common Core Connection (CCSS.Math.Content.7.RP.A.2)

Grade: Seventh

Domain: Ratios and Proportional Relationships

Cluster:

Analyze proportional relationships and use them to solve real-world and mathematical problems.

2. Recognize and represent proportional relationships between quantities.

   a. Decide whether two quantities are in a proportional relationship, e.g., by testing for equivalent ratios in a table or graphing on a coordinate plan and observing whether the graph is a straight line through the origin.

Uncovering Student Understanding About the Key Concepts

Using the Best Estimates: Solving Proportions Probe can provide the following information about how the students are thinking about equivalent ratios.

Do they

- recognize this as a problem involving equivalent ratios?

- use estimation strategies such as rounding up or down?

- understand the problem as a multiplicative relationship between two quantities?

OR

Do they

- see it as two fractions unrelated to each other?

- try to mentally calculate the answer by cross multiplication and division?

- see it as a problem with an additive relationship?

Exploring Excerpts From Educational Resources and Related Research

Common areas of difficulty for students:

Students lack concrete and visual conceptions of proportion and size. (Stepans, Schmidt, Welsh, Reins, & Saigo, 2005, p. 53)

Students' ability to relate fraction notation to ratios impedes their ability to use fractions. . . . Students have difficulty with scaling activities largely because they learn fractions in isolation. (Stepans et al., 2005, pp. 53–54)

Students tend to see problems in terms of either-or relationships; that is, either the quantities are the same or they are different. However, many different ratios can be proportional because the relationship between the two pairs of numbers is the same. . . . Even students who can generate sets of equivalent fractions often have difficulty recognizing the invariance in equivalent ratios. (Langrall & Swafford, 2000, p. 259)

Surveying the Prompts and Selected Responses in the Probe

The Probe consists of two separate selected response items. The prompts and selected responses are designed to elicit understandings and common difficulties as described below:

If a student chooses	It is likely that the student
1b or 2a (correct answers)	• is using multiplicative reasoning within or between the ratios [See Sample Student Response 1]. • is accurately rounding up or down then solving for x [See Sample Student Response 2]. *Look for indication of the student's understanding in the written explanations of how the student got the answer.*
1a or 2c	• is using additive reasoning within or between the ratios instead of multiplicative reasoning [See Sample Student Response 3].
Other various answers	• is incorrectly applying an algorithm [See Sample Student Response 4]; or • made a calculation error [See Sample Student Response 5].

Teaching Implications and Considerations

Ideas for eliciting more information from students about their understanding and difficulties:

- What strategy can you use to estimate with decimals?
- How will estimating the decimals help with understanding the ratio? The proportion?
- What numbers are you going to compare to find *x*? Why?
- Are there more than one set of numbers you can compare to find the scale?

Ideas for planning instruction in response to what you learned from the results of administering the Probe:

- Students should be given numerous activities with estimation. They should be able to estimate the answer before finding it to be able to check for accuracy.
- "Formally setting up proportions using variables and applying the cross-product rule should be delayed until after students have had an opportunity to build on their informal knowledge and develop an understanding of the essential components of proportional reasoning" (Langrall & Swafford, 2000, p. 261).
- Students should understand that there is a multiplicative relationship within ratios and between two ratios in a proportion.
- Use similar figures through diagrams, manipulatives, and technology to investigate the many relationships within and between the ratios.
- Allow students to compare and contrast proportional and nonproportional objects and ratios.

Sample Student Responses to Best Estimates: Solving Proportions

Responses That Suggest Understanding

Sample Student Response 1

Probe Item 1. b. By looking at the 1st ratio you can tell it's about 3 to 1 with the smaller number on the bottom so with 7 on the bottom, multiply it by 3 and you get 21.

Probe Item 2. a. By looking at the 2nd ration you can say it's about 2 to 8 or 1 to 4. Now the smaller number is in the top so 1 x 4 is 4.

Sample Student Response 2

Probe Item 1. b. First round all the numbers. $\frac{15}{5} = \frac{x}{7}$. Set up the cross *x* and 5*x* = 15 × 7 or 5*x* = 105. $\frac{105}{5}$ = 21.

Responses That Suggest Difficulty

Sample Student Response 3

Probe Item 1. a. Look across from 4.8 to 7.4 which is about 3. 3 more than 15 is 18.

Sample Student Response 4

Probe Item 1. c. $5 \times 7 = 35$. $\frac{35}{15}$ is 2. Smallest number there is 10.

Sample Student Response 5:

Probe Item 2. a. $8.3 \times 1.2 = 108.6$ 100 divided by 2.5 is about 4.

Proportional Reasoning Sort

Reproducible student cards and Recording Sheet follow Teacher Notes on p. 85

	Proportional	Not Proportional

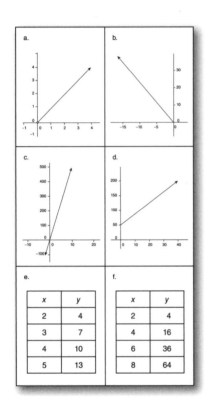

g.

Input	Output
5	40
10	80
15	100
20	120

h.

# Items	Price
1	$2.50
2	$5.00
3	$7.50
4	$10.00

m.

$$y = -\frac{3}{5}x$$

n.

$$2x + y = 2$$

i.

Two friends were meeting at the pool to swim laps. Sam got there first and swam 4 laps before Michelle joined. If they continue together swimming at the same pace of 0.8 laps per minute, how many laps would Sam and Michelle each swim in 10 minutes? 20 minues? 40 minutes?

j.

David has several books to read in preparation for his research paper. David read 40 pages of a book in 50 minutes. How many pages should he be able to read in 80 minutes? 120 minutes? 20 minutes?

o.

$$x = 8$$

p.

$$y = 2x$$

k.

Fourteen students assembled 80 care packages for a school care drive. They decided to get more students involved to create additional packages. How many care packages can 90 students make? 100? 120?

l.

$$y = \frac{2}{3}x + 5$$

q.

$$x = 2y$$

r.

$$y = \frac{x}{3}$$

Advance Preparation: Create cards by photocopying on card stock and cutting. Separate the two blank cards and the two label cards from the deck and shuffle the rest of the cards.

Instructions:

1. Invite the student(s) to sort the cards into two piles: **Proportional** and **Not Proportional**. Use the label cards to identify the piles.

2. As students finish the sort, give them the blank cards and ask them to create their own **Proportional** and **Not Proportional** examples (two of each).

3. Either choose three cards for the student or ask the student to choose three cards from the **Proportional** pile. Ask her to explain how she knew these cards should go in the **Proportional** pile.

4. Either choose three cards for the student or ask the student to choose three cards from the **Not Proportional** pile. Ask him to explain how he knew these cards should go in the **Not Proportional** pile. Use the recording sheet as appropriate.

Teacher Notes: Proportional Reasoning Sort

Questions to Consider About the Key Mathematical Concepts

When solving problems involving proportional reasoning, can students distinguish between proportional and nonproportional relationships? To what extent do they

- make sense of proportional and nonproportional data given in various forms?
- model proportional reasoning by describing proportional characteristics and finding the constant of proportionality?
- describe how they decided which cards to place in each category (proportional or nonproportional)?

Common Core Connection (CCSS.Math.Content.7.RP.A.2)

Grade: Seventh

Domain: Ratios and Proportional Relationships

Cluster:

Analyze proportional relationships and use them to solve real-world and mathematical problems.

2. Recognize and represent proportional relationships between quantities.

   a. Decide whether two quantities are in a proportional relationship (e.g., by testing for equivalent ratios in a table or graphing on a coordinate plane and observing whether the graph is a straight line through the origin).

   b. Identify the constant of proportionality (unit rate) in tables, graphs, equations, diagrams, and verbal descriptions of proportional relationships.

   c. Represent proportional relationships by equations. For example, if total cost t is proportional to the number n of items purchased at a constant price p, the relationship between the total cost and the number of items can be expressed as $t = pn$.

Uncovering Student Understanding About the Key Concepts

Using the Proportional Reasoning Sort Probe can provide the following information about how the students are thinking about proportional reasoning.

Do they

- recognize the graphical characteristics of proportional relationships?

OR

Do they

- describe all lines as proportional?

- understand how to find the initial values and rate of change given a graph, equation, table, or verbal description of two quantities?

OR

- lack understanding of the information needed or the process of finding the initial values and rate of change between two quantities?

- understand how to reason about the relationships in verbal descriptions?

OR

- get confused with the words describing the relationship?

Variation: Is It a Proportional Relationship? Justified List

*E*xploring Excerpts From Educational Resources and Related Research

Common areas of difficulty for students:

Mathematics educators agree that ratio and proportion are important middle school mathematics topics. In fact, researchers have stated that proportional reasoning involves "watershed concepts" that are at the "cornerstone of higher mathematics" (Lamon 1994; Lesh, Post, and Behr 1988). Yet assisting students in developing robust understanding of the many concepts and procedures that are related to using ratios, rates, and proportions is not straightforward. For example, being able to reason proportionally and being able to represent that reasoning symbolically do not always go hand-in-hand. As with many complex topics, students' understanding grows with time and experience. (Chapin & Anderson, 2003, p. 420)

A common error in setting up proportions is placing numbers in incorrect locations. This is especially easy to do when the order in which quantities are stated in the problem is switched within the problem statement. (Common Core Standards Writing Team, 2011b, p. xx)

*S*urveying the Prompts and Selected Responses in the Probe

The Probe consists of a set of examples and nonexamples card sort. The prompts and selected responses are designed to elicit understandings and common difficulties as described in the following table:

If a student chooses	It is likely that the student
Yes for a, b, c, h, j, m, p, q, r No for d, e, f, g, i, k, l, n, o (correct answers)	• understands that if a relationship is proportional, its graph will be a straight line and pass through the origin. The student recognizes proportional relationships in equations, tables, and verbal descriptions in which there is a constant ratio (rate of change, constant of proportionality) between two quantities (two quantities vary together) [See Sample Student Response 1]. *Look for indication of the student's understanding in the written explanations of how the student got the answer.*

Various incorrect placements	• does not recognize proportional relationship in one or more of the following ways:
	  o thinks all linear relationships are proportional [See Sample Student Response 2];
	  o assumes a constant rate of change [See Sample Student Response 3];
	  o may not recognize the proportional relationship when given a form other than $y = mx + b$ [See Sample Student Response 4].

Note: Some websites and curricula place relationships with negative rates of change in the **Not Proportional** Category. Review your local context before using the Probe with students.

Teaching Implications and Considerations

Ideas for eliciting more information from students about their understanding and difficulties:

- How do you find a constant of proportionality (rate of change) for a graph, equation, table, or verbal description?
- When x goes up by one, what happens to y in the graph? the equation? the table? the verbal description?
- Can you write a sentence in your own words about the change in y when x changes one unit?
- What is the value of the output (y) when the input (x) is 0? What does this tell us graphically? Do the lines of the graphs go through the origin? What does this tell us about the data?

Ideas for planning instruction in response to what you learned from the results of administering the Probe:

- As students work with proportional relationships, they [should] write equations of the form $y = cx$, where c is a constant of proportionality, i.e., a unit rate. They [should] see this unit rate as the amount of increase in y as x increases by 1 unit in a ratio table and they [should] recognize the unit rate as the vertical increase in a "unit rate triangle" or "slope triangle" with horizontal side of length 1 for a graph of a proportional relationship. (Progressions for the Common Core State Standards for Mathematics [draft] The Common Core Standards Writing Team, 2011b)

- According to Van de Walle, "Proportional Reasoning is usually taught in grades 6 to 9. When students are taught this concept at earlier grades, they may not be ready. This encourages students to apply rules without thinking. When this happens, the ability to reason proportionally often does not develop" (Van de Walle, 2007, p. 355).

Sample Student Responses to Proportional Reasoning Sort

Responses That Suggest Understanding

Sample Student Response 1

The graphs were the easiest. I looked for the line going through (0,0) and a straight line. The equations were next easiest since I can tell right away if there is a slope and no b (because that means 0). Next I looked at the tables and kept going backwards until I saw whether $x = 0$ and $y = 0$. The stories were somewhat harder since I had to imagine the graph and then decide if it said enough about things at the same rate of speed.

Responses That Suggest Difficulty

Sample Student Response 2

Anything that forms a straight line is proportional. I made a graph for each card. Line was yes and not straight line was no.

Sample Student Response 3

We learned that proportional means constant rate of change and 0 as the y-intercept. *The student misplaced* k, *and when asked about it replied,* I used a rate of $\frac{80}{14}$.

Sample Student Response 4

For the equations, I picked everything that had both an x or a y but no + or − number with them

Proportional Relationship Card Sort

a.

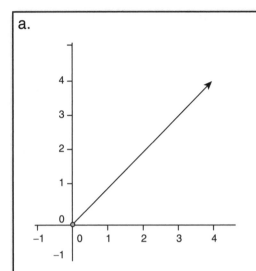

b.

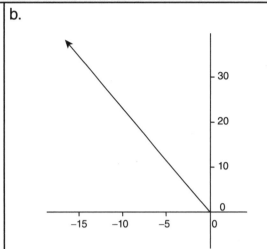

c.

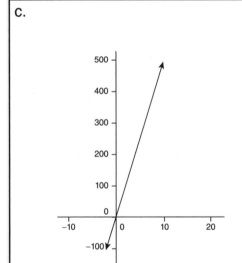

d.

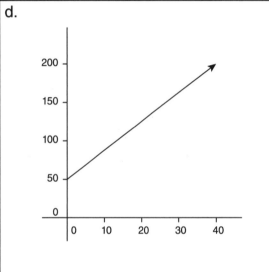

e.

x	y
2	4
3	7
4	10
5	13

f.

x	y
2	4
4	16
6	36
8	64

g.

Input	Output
5	40
10	80
15	100
20	120

h.

# Items	Price
1	$2.50
2	$5.00
3	$7.50
4	$10.00

i.

Two friends were meeting at the pool to swim laps. Sam got there first and swam 4 laps before Michelle joined her. If they continue together swimming at the same pace of 0.8 laps per minute, how many laps would Sam and Michelle each swim in 10 minutes? 20 minutes? 40 minutes?

j.

David has several books to read in preparation for his research paper. David reads 40 pages of a book in 50 minutes. At this rate, how many pages should he be able to read in 80 minutes? In 120 minutes? In 20 minutes?

k.

Fourteen students assembled 80 care packages for a school community service project. They decided to get more students involved to create additional packages. How many care packages can 90 students make? 100 students? 120 students?

l.

$$y = \frac{2}{3}x + 5$$

m.

$$y = -\frac{3}{5}x$$

n.

$$2x + y = 2$$

o.

$$x = 8$$

p.

$$y = 2x$$

q.

$$x = 2y$$

r.

$$y = \frac{x}{3}$$

Proportional	Not Proportional

Recording Sheet: Number Sort

Proportional Cards	Explanation
Not Proportional Cards	**Explanation**

Variation: Is It a Proportional Relationship?

Determine whether each of the following represents a linear function.

Circle the correct answer.	Explain your choice.
1. a. Yes b. No c. Not enough information	
2. $$y = -\frac{3}{5}x$$ a. Yes b. No c. Not enough information	
3. <table><tr><th>x</th><th>y</th></tr><tr><td>2</td><td>4</td></tr><tr><td>3</td><td>7</td></tr><tr><td>4</td><td>10</td></tr><tr><td>5</td><td>13</td></tr></table> a. Yes b. No c. Not enough information	

Circle the correct answer.	Explain your choice.
4. $$x = 2y$$ a. Yes b. No c. Not enough information	
5. 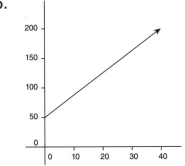 a. Yes b. No c. Not enough information	
6. | # Items	Price
1	$2.50
2	$5.00
3	$7.50
4	$10.00 | a. Yes b. No c. Not enough information	

4

Expressions and Equations and Functions Probes

The content of the Probes in this chapter aligns with the standards for Grades 6 through 8. The Probes will also be relevant beyond the aligned grade level for students in higher grades who have not yet met standards from previous grade levels as well as for students who have already met the standards at their own grade level.

We developed these Probes to address this critical area of focus for middle school students, described in the standards (CCSSO, 2010) as follows:

- Apply and extend previous understandings of arithmetic to algebraic expressions.

> The content of the Probes in this chapter aligns with the standards for Grades 6 through 8. The Probes will also be relevant beyond the aligned grade level for students in higher grades who have not yet met standards from previous grade levels as well as for students who have already met the standards at their own grade level.

- Reason about and solve one-variable equations and inequalities.
- Represent and analyze quantitative relationships between dependent and independent variables.
- Use properties of operations to generate equivalent expressions.
- Solve real-life and mathematical problems using numerical and algebraic expressions and equations.

- Work with radicals and integer exponents.
- Understand the connections between proportional relationships, lines, and linear equations.
- Analyze and solve linear equations and pairs of simultaneous linear equations.
- Define, evaluate, and compare functions.
- Use functions to model relationships between quantities.

Common Core Math Content

Common Core Mathematical Content	Related Question	Probe Name
Use variables to represent quantities in a real-world or mathematical problem, and construct simple equations and inequalities to solve problems by reasoning about the quantities. CCSS.Math.Content.7.EE.B.4	When solving problems involving operations with integers, can students generalize the results of an operation when given constraints about the numbers to be operated on?	Value of the Inequality (p. 94)
Use variables to represent quantities in a real-world or mathematical problem, and construct simple equations and inequalities to solve problems by reasoning about the quantities. CCSS.Math.Content.7.EE.B.4	When solving problems involving symbolic (algebraic) representation, can students make sense of relationships being described?	Writing Equations (p. 100)
Know and apply the properties of integer exponents to generate equivalent numerical expressions. CCSS.Math.Content.8.EE.A.1	When solving problems involving integers, variables, and exponents, can students use properties of exponents to correctly simplify expressions?	Is It Equivalent? (p. 105)
Interpret the equation $y = mx + b$ as defining a linear function, whose graph is a straight line; give examples of functions that are not linear. CCSS.Math.Content.8.F.A.3	When solving problems involving linear relationships, can students determine equivalent forms of representation?	Linear Equations (p. 109)
Determine the rate of change and initial value of the function from a description of a relationship or from two (x, y) values, including reading these from a table or from a graph. CCSS.Math.Content.8.F.B.4	When solving problems involving equations and tables, can students interpret key features to determine whether they represent a linear function?	Is It a Linear Function? (p. 114)

Value of the Inequality

4.1

If $m > 0$ and $n < 0$, decide if each inequality is *Always True, Sometimes True, Never True*, or *Can't Be Determined* with the given information.

Circle the correct answer.	Justify your choice.
1. $m + n < 0$ a. Always True b. Sometimes True c. Never True d. Can't Be Determined	
2. $m - n > 0$ a. Always True b. Sometimes True c. Never True d. Can't Be Determined	
3. $(m)(n) < 0$ a. Always True b. Sometimes True c. Never True d. Can't Be Determined	
4. $\dfrac{m}{n} > 0$ a. Always True b. Sometimes True c. Never True d. Can't Be Determined	

Teacher Notes: Value of the Inequality

Questions to Consider About the Key Mathematical Concepts

When solving problems involving operations with integers, can students generalize the results of an operation when given constraints about the numbers to be operated on? To what extent do they

- make sense of the properties of operations?
- interpret an algebraic inequality?
- use examples and counter-examples to justify their choice?

Common Core Connection (CCSS.Math.Content.7.NS.A.1; CCSS.Math.Content.7.NS.A.2; CCSS.Math.Content.7.EE.B.4)

Grade: Seventh

Domain: The Number System

Cluster:

Apply and extend previous understandings of operations with fractions to add, subtract, multiply, and divide rational numbers.

1. Apply and extend previous understandings of addition and subtraction to add and subtract rational numbers; represent addition and subtraction on a horizontal or vertical number line diagram.

2. Apply and extend previous understandings of multiplication and division and of fractions to multiply and divide rational numbers.

Domain: Expressions and Equations

Cluster:

Solve real-life and mathematical problems using numerical and algebraic expressions and equations.

4. Use variables to represent quantities in a real-world or mathematical problem, and construct simple equations and inequalities to solve problems by reasoning about the quantities.

Uncovering Student Understanding About the Key Concepts

Using the Value of the Inequality Probe can provide the following information about how the students are thinking about operating with integers through the interpretation of inequalities.

Do they

- correctly apply the rules of operating on integers?

- correctly interpret the inequalities, first in the numbers involved and second in the results of the operations?

- use properties of operations to justify a choice of "always true" and "never true"?

- use examples and counter-examples to justify a choice of "sometimes true"?

OR

OR

OR

OR

Do they

- overgeneralize rules from one operation to another?

- have difficulty determining either the values of *m* and/ or *n* or the value of the resulting operation?

- use only examples or counter-examples?

- rely on only examples or only counter-examples when both are needed?

Exploring Excerpts From Educational Resources and Related Research

Common areas of difficulty for students:

Data from the Mathematics Assessment for Learning and Teaching (MaLT) project data base indicate that students demonstrate the following types of difficulties with integer operation problems: the sign and the number conceived of as two separate objects, ignoring the negative sign, viewing the division symbol as "subtract." (Ryan & Williams, 2007, p. 218)

Relatively few students displayed understanding of integers. They tend to memorize "rules" given by their teachers. Students often struggle to remember all the different rules, and even if they could remember rules, they were often not sure which rule applied to which task. The study also found:

- Students got mixed-up with operation and signs when there are subtraction and negative signs in a problem.
- Some students' errors are a mixture of many types of errors:
  ○ They take the sign of the larger number and put it in front and multiplied the sign of the numbers to get the operations.
  ○ They apply multiplication rule every time they saw two signs.
  ○ They also take the sign of the larger number and then subtract or add the rest.

- Students generally do better in multiplication and division of integers compared to addition and subtraction involving negative integers. This can be due to confusion because there are two signs of the same kind in a problem involving subtraction. It can also be due to the multiplication rule as being easier to remember. (Kahlid, Rosmah, & Badarudin, 2012, slide 15)

Surveying the Prompts and Selected Responses in the Probe

The Probe consists of four related justified list items. The prompts and selected responses are designed to elicit understandings and common difficulties as described below:

If a student chooses	It is likely that the student
1b, 2a, 3a, 4c (correct answers)	• correctly interpreted the values of m and n; and applied the properties of operating with integers [See Sample Student Responses 1, 2, and 3]. *Look for indication of the student's understanding in the written explanations of how the student got the answer.*
1a	• has overgeneralized the rule for multiplication and division—"a negative and a positive is always a negative" [See Sample Student Response 7].
2b	• has dropped the negative sign associated with $n < 0$ and is not interpreting the operation in terms of subtracting a negative [See Sample Student Response 4].
3b, 4b	• has overgeneralized the rule for addition—"take the sign of the larger" [See Sample Student Responses 4, 5, and 6].
Various other choices	• can apply properties for some operations but not others; or • has misinterpreted the value of m or n therefore choosing incorrectly about the value of the operation [See Sample Student Responses 5, 6, and 7].

Teaching Implications and Considerations

Ideas for eliciting more information from students about their understanding and difficulties:

- What does this inequality symbol mean? Can you give me an example of an integer that makes that inequality true?
- How do you substitute values for m and n in the inequality?
- How can you justify your choice using what you know about the properties of operating on integers rather than just providing examples?

Ideas for planning instruction in response to what you learned from the results of administering the Probe:

- Build foundational understanding of the meaning of and notations for negative numbers.
- Canceling a debt has powerful meaning behind subtracting a negative number for most students. They often relate to money and understand discussions based on it.
- Build in multiple opportunities for students to model operations with integers using chip models and number lines. Do not jump too quickly to rules such as "subtracting a negative is the same as adding a positive." Instead allow the students to form these generalizations based on modeling both processes numerous times.
- Use problem contexts and ask students to develop their own problems to represent a given numerical equation.
- Support the connection between the modeling of integer operations and the mathematical model (e.g., numerical equations).
- Help students form generalizations and represent those generalizations with algebraic equations and inequalities.

Sample Student Responses to Value of the Inequality

Responses That Suggest Understanding

Sample Student Response 1

Probe Item 1. b. If m has a greater absolute value than n, it is true. If not, it is false.

Probe Item 2. a. A positive minus a negative is always a positive.

Probe Item 3. a. A positive times a negative is always a negative.

Probe Item 4. c. A positive divided by a negative equals a negative.

Sample Student Response 2

Probe Item 1. b. A positive plus a negative takes the positive number down, but not always below zero. Ex: $2 - 4 < 0$ would be true, $4 - 2 < 0$ would not be true.

Sample Student Response 3:

Probe Item 1. b. It will totally depend on which one is farther away from zero.

Responses That Suggest Difficulty

Sample Student Response 4

Probe Item 2. b. This could be either positive or negative, depending on which numbers are chosen for m and n.

Probe Item 4. b. This also depends on the numbers chosen . . . it could be either positive or negative.

Sample Student Response 5

Probe Item 1. c. If something larger than zero is added to something smaller than zero the result will still be larger than zero, not smaller.

Probe Item 3. d. This can't be determined without knowing what m or n are.

Sample Student Response 6

Probe Item 1. c. If $m > 0$, then $m + n$ isn't possibly less than 0.

Sample Student Response 7

Probe Item 1. a. When adding a number that is greater than zero to a number that is not, the answer is always less than zero.

Probe Item 2. b. When subtracting a number that is greater than zero from one that is not, the answer is almost always positive.

Sample Student Response 8

Probe Item 1. a. If $m = 1$ and $n = -20$ then yes.

Probe Item 2. b. If $m = 1$ and $n = -5$, then yes.

Writing Equations

4.2

Choose the equation that best represents the statement. In each equation *s* represents the number of students and *t* represents the number of teachers.

Circle the correct answer.	Explain your choice.
1. **There are 45 more students than teachers on the field trip.** a. $45 = s + t$ b. $s + 45 = t$ c. $t + 45 = s$	
2. **There are 7 times as many students as teachers in the cafeteria today.** a. $7s = t$ b. $7t = s$ c. $st = 7$	
3. **There are 17 fewer teachers than students in the gym.** a. $17 - t = s$ b. $t - s = 17$ c. $s - t = 17$	

Teacher Notes: Writing Equations

Questions to Consider About the Key Mathematical Concepts

When solving problems involving symbolic (algebraic) representation, can students make sense of relationships being described? To what extent do they

- make sense of words describing a real-world linear relationship?
- model the use of variables and equations to represent linear relationships?
- describe the reasoning behind their placement of the numbers and variables?

Common Core Connection (CCSS.Math.Content.7.EE.B.4)

Grade: Seventh

Domain: Expressions and Equations

Cluster:

Solve real-life and mathematical problems using numerical and algebraic expressions and equations.

4. Use variables to represent quantities in a real-world or mathematical problem, and construct simple equations and inequalities to solve problems by reasoning about the quantities.

Uncovering Student Understanding About the Key Concepts

Using the Writing Equations Probe can provide the following information about how the students are thinking about symbolic representation of a linear relationship.

Do they
- write an equation based on the relationship described?

OR

Do they
- write an equation with numbers and letters (variables) in the order in which they appear in the description (direct translation)?

Do they

- understand the mathematical meaning and representation of the words used?

- use variables to replace the number of students and teachers?

Do they

OR • misrepresent the words with inaccurate mathematical operations?

OR • use variables to replace the word "student" or "teacher"?

Exploring Excerpts From Educational Resources and Related Research

Common areas of difficulty for students:

Many students have difficulty forming equations and symbolic expressions that model worded problem statements. They cannot attach meaning to algebraic expressions. (Stepans et al., 2005, p. 150)

Students have difficulty distinguishing between constants and variables. [They] are confused by the different roles of letters in expressions. (Stepans et al., 2005, p. 150)

[There are] multiple ways in which students are asked to use letters [in algebra, causing] difficulties in sorting them out. Students have difficulties knowing when a letter is part of a word and when it is a mathematical variable. (NCTM, 2003, p. 140)

Surveying the Prompts and Selected Responses in the Probe

The Probe consists of three separate selected response items. The prompts and selected responses are designed to elicit understandings and common difficulties as described below.

If a student chooses	It is likely that the student
1c, 2b, 3c (correct answers)	• understands that variables represent numbers. The student can accurately make sense of the words and mathematical relationships to write equations to represent the statements [See Sample Student Response 1]. *Look for indication of the student's understanding in the written explanations of how the student got the answer.*
1b, 2a, 3a	• is using a direct translation of the words without understanding the relationship being described between the variables. The student is likely using the variables to represent words instead of the number of teachers and students [See Sample Student Responses 2 and 3].
1a, 2c, 3b	• is guessing and is not reasoning about the statements given [See Sample Student Response 4].

*T*eaching Implications and Considerations

Ideas for eliciting more information from students about their understanding and difficulties:

- Can you describe the relationship in your own words?
- What variables are you going to use? What do the variables represent (the number of . . .)?
- What do the words "more," "less," and "is" mean mathematically? What do the phrases "times as many" and "less than" mean mathematically?
- Is there a variable that is dependent on the other one?
- Is the equation you wrote balanced? Tell me how you know it is.
- Is there any other way the relationship can be expressed symbolically (algebraically)?

Ideas for planning instruction in response to what you learned from the results of administering the Probe:

- Have students define variables.
- Provide opportunities for students to interpret relationships among quantities in a variety of contexts before working with variables in equations.
- The concept of a variable should be grounded in real-world situations familiar and interesting to students before being defined abstractly.
- Allow students to use other forms of representation (tables and graphs) to verify accuracy of their algebraic representation.
- Provide students with a list of words that are commonly used for mathematical relationships. Have individuals, groups, or the class compile mathematical operations or symbols that have the same meaning as the words and that are frequently used in symbolic representations.
- When possible, use visual tools and technology to aid the concrete thinkers in the abstract process of symbolic representation.

Sample Student Responses to Writing Equations

Responses That Suggest Understanding

Sample Student Response 1

Probe Item 1. I thought about an example first. What if 1 teacher. Then there would be have to be 46 students. $1 + 45 = 46$ so $t + 45 = s$.

Probe Item 2. My example is for 2 teachers this time. 2 teachers × 7 would be 14 students so $t \times 7 = s$.

Probe Item 3. Using 3 for teachers 3 + 17 would be 20 so $t + 17 = s$. Another way of rearranging this would be $20 - 3 = 17$ or $s - t = 17$.

Responses That Suggest Difficulty

Sample Student Response 2

Probe Item 2. The $7t = s$ shows just what the words said.

Sample Student Response 3

Probe Item 3. Less means minus and 17 less means 17 minus so $17 - t = s$ fits the problem best.

Sample Student Response 4

Probe Item 3. Like I said before. They all look the same with a t and s and a $-$ and $=$ and a 17 so I just circled one of them.

Is It Equivalent?

4.3

Determine whether the expressions are equivalent.

Circle Yes or No.	Explain your choice.
1. a. $3p^3q^2(4p^2q^4)$ b. $12p^6q^8$ Yes No	
2. a. $(3x^2)^4$ b. $3x^8$ Yes No	
3. a. $5a^{-2}b(-2ab^3)$ b. $\dfrac{-10b^4}{a}$ Yes No	
4. a. $-5m^{-3}(-4m^{-2})$ b. $\dfrac{4m^2}{5m^3}$ Yes No	

Teacher Notes: Is It Equivalent?

Questions to Consider About the Key Mathematical Concepts

When solving problems involving integers, variables, and exponents, can students use properties of exponents to correctly simplify expressions? To what extent do they

- make sense of the properties of exponents?
- model understanding of the meaning and effects of arithmetic operations with integers, variables, and exponents?
- describe their reasoning and process used to determine equivalency?

Common Core Connection (CCSS.Math.Content.8.EE.A.1)

Grade: Eighth

Domain: Expressions and Equations

Cluster:

Work with radicals and integer exponents.

1. Know and apply the properties of integer exponents to generate equivalent numerical expressions.

Uncovering Student Understanding About the Key Concepts

Using the Is It Equivalent? Probe can provide the following information about how the students are thinking about simplifying expressions involving variables with exponents.

Do they
- correctly add powers when multiplying variables with the same base and multiply powers when raising a power to a power?

- distribute a power completely when parentheses are being used?

- have an understanding of negative powers and rewrite them using positive powers?

Do they
OR • multiply the powers when multiplying and/or add powers when raising powers to powers?

OR • forget to distribute the power to the coefficient of an expression?

OR • confuse a negative power with a negative integer?

Exploring Excerpts From Educational Resources and Related Research

Common areas of difficulty for students:

In mathematical equations [and expressions], the signals for ordering are not those of ordinary language. They include parentheses (which are not used as we are using them here in the ordinary language way) and more subtle signals that must be deduced from a knowledge of formal rules for the procedures of operations. Natural-language rules are no help in reading mathematical expressions. (NCTM, 1999, p. 311)

Surveying the Prompts and Selected Responses in the Probe

The Probe consists of four separate selected response items. The prompts and selected responses are designed to elicit understandings and common difficulties as described below:

If a student chooses	It is likely that the student
1 No, 2 No, 3 Yes, 4 No (correct answers)	• has an understanding of the properties of exponents and how to use them to simplify expressions [See Sample Student Responses 1 and 2]. *Look for indication of the student's understanding in the written explanations of how the student got the answer.*
1 Yes, 2 Yes, 3 No, 4 Yes	• has a lack of conceptual and/or procedural understanding of the properties of exponents. Many students confuse properties they have learned and overgeneralize rules and shortcuts [See Sample Student Responses 3 and 4].

Teaching Implications and Considerations

Ideas for eliciting more information from students about their understanding and difficulties:

- Can you verbalize what the expressions mean? (Can the students verbalize all of the operations accurately?)
- Can you expand this power? How can you use the expanded version to help with simplification?
- Ask students about specific properties of exponents and what they mean mathematically.
- If you were to replace the given variables with numbers in each expression, then do the computations, which would produce the same answer?

Ideas for planning instruction in response to what you learned from the results of administering the Probe:

- Have student discuss the conceptual meaning of using powers and allow them to discover the properties (rules, shortcuts) on their own so that they can have the actual mathematical meaning in place first.
- Encourage students to substitute numbers for variables in each expression to see if the proposed simplification produces an equivalent answer.
- Give students extensive opportunities to explore different representations of exponential expressions. Provide examples of equivalent and nonequivalent expressions for the basis of conversations around the meaning of exponents.
- Allow opportunities to compare and analyze the advantages and disadvantages of different representations of the same expression.

Sample Student Responses to Is It Equivalent?

Responses That Suggest Understanding

Sample Student Response 1

Probe Item 1. No. When you add the exponents for p, it comes out to 5 not 6. Also when you add the exponents for q, it comes out to 6 not 8. It looks like they were multiplying instead of adding, which is wrong.

Probe Item 3. Yes. Item a comes out to having a negative exponent ($-2 + 1 = -1$) so you put it in the denominator with a positive exponent.

Sample Student Response 2

Probe Item 1. No. When you add the exponents and multiply the numbers out front, they are not equal to each other.

Probe Item 2. No. Because the exponent is outside the parentheses, it has to be distributed into the 3 too.

Probe Item 4. No. The problems don't look anything like each other. There needs to be a 20 in the numerator and the m^5 in the denominator (or keep it in the numerator but make the 5 a negative).

Responses That Suggest Difficulty

Sample Student Response 3

Probe Item 1. Yes $3 \cdot 4 = 12$, $p^3 \cdot p^2 = p^6$, and $q^2 \cdot q^4 = q^8$.

Probe Item 3. No. The -10 should go down with the a.

Probe Item 4. Yes. Just flip the equation so it becomes positive.

Sample Student Response 4

Probe Item 2. Yes. 2 times 4 is 8 so this would be correct.

Probe Item 4. No. The equations would end up being $\frac{1}{20} m^5$.

Linear Equations

Determine whether each equation could represent Line a.

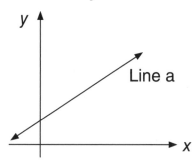

1. $y = \dfrac{2}{3}x + 5$ Circle One: Yes   No   Can't Determine

Explain your choice:

2. $y = -6x + 2$ Circle One: Yes   No   Can't Determine

Explain your choice:

3. $y = 15x + 45$ Circle One: Yes   No   Can't Determine

Explain your choice:

4. $-4x = y + 2$ Circle One: Yes   No   Can't Determine

Explain your choice:

5. $2x + 3y = 6$ Circle One: Yes   No   Can't Determine

Explain your choice:

Teacher Notes: Linear Equations

Questions to Consider About the Key Mathematical Concepts

When solving problems involving linear relationships, can students determine equivalent forms of representation? To what extent do they

- make sense of information given in graphical and symbolic forms?
- model reasoning skills that allow them to determine whether different representations are equivalent?
- describe key features of graphs and equations that allow analysis of equivalency?

Common Core Connection (CCSS.Math.Content.8.F.A.3)

Grade: Eighth

Domain: Functions

Cluster:

Define, evaluate, and compare functions.

3. Interpret the equation $y = mx + b$ as defining a linear function, whose graph is a straight line; give examples of functions that are not linear. For example, the function $A = s^2$ giving the area of a square as a function of its side length is not linear because its graph contains the points (1,1), (2,4), and (3,9), which are not on a straight line.

Uncovering Student Understanding About the Key Concepts

Using the Linear Equations Probe can provide the following information about how the students are thinking about multiple representations of linear functions.

Do they
- look for relevant information shown in the graph that will help match an equation (rate of change and *y*-intercept)?

OR

Do they
- not see the relationship between a graph and its equation?

Do they
- recognize key features of linear equations when written in various forms?

OR

Do they
- not use the numbers in the equations as clues to what the graph would look like?

- consider how the sizes of the intervals would change the appearance of the line?

OR

- determine slope by thinking only about intervals of 1 unit?

Exploring Excerpts From Educational Resources and Related Research

Common areas of difficulty for students:

Students fail to recognize the underlying equivalence when the same set of points is represented by a graph or an equation or a table. They tend to see changes in form as producing unrelated representations. (NCTM, 1999, p. 215)

Students may not see the links between different representations of a functional relation—for example, the mutual dependence between a function's graph and equation, or between its table and equation. (Driscoll, 1999, p. 146)

Surveying the Prompts and Selected Responses in the Probe

The Probe consists of five selected response items each relating to a common graph. The prompts and selected responses are designed to elicit understandings and common difficulties as described below:

If a student chooses	It is likely that the student
1. yes, 2. no, 3. yes, 4. no, 5. yes (correct answers)	• recognizes multiple ways of representing linear functions. [See Sample Student Response 1]. *Look for indication of the student's understanding in the written explanations of how the student got the answer.*
Various other patterns	• fails to recognize one or more of the following key features of equations and graphs that link them together as representing the same information: ○ positive slope versus positive coefficient of x [See Sample Student Response 2]; ○ positive y-intercept versus positive constant [See Sample Student Response 2];

(Continued)

(Continued)

If a student chooses	It is likely that the student
	○ magnitude of the slope depends on the intervals not the "look" of the graph [See Sample Student Response 3]; or ○ various other incorrect ideas [See Sample Student Response 4].

Teaching Implications and Considerations

Ideas for eliciting more information from students about their understanding and difficulties:

- What information is shown in the graph that can help determine a possible equation?
- What are some key features of the equations that might help you graph them?
- What do the numbers tell you in the equation?
- Does the graph have a positive or negative rate of change? How can you find the rate of change in the equations?
- Where does the graph cross the *y*-axis? What would the *x* value be at this point? How would you determine the *y*-intercept in an equation?

Ideas for planning instruction in response to what you learned from the results of administering the Probe:

- Allow students ample opportunities to explore the explicit connections between, and solve problems in which they use, tables, graphs, words, and symbolic representations.
- "Students should see algebra not just as the process of transforming and manipulating symbols but rather as a tool for expressing and analyzing relationships between quantities that change" (NCTM, 1999, p. 215).
- Have students explore the advantages and disadvantage of representing a relationship with each of the different types of representation.
- Use technology as an avenue for students to make connections between the different types of representations.

Sample Student Responses to Linear Equations

Responses That Suggest Understanding

Sample Student Response 1

Probe Item 1. Yes. Since I don't see labels on the axis, the numbers there could be anything. I know the slope is up to right (pos) and the line crosses *y* at a pos number.

Probe Item 2. No. Negative slope means up and to left.

Probe Item 3. Yes. Pos slope and pos *y*-intercept.

Probe Item 4. No. I changed to *y* = form so I could tell if slope was pos and *y*-inter pos. Slope was neg.

Probe Item 5. Yes. Same thing. This time both were pos.

Responses That Suggest Difficulty

Sample Student Response 2

Probe Item. d. The *x* number is +4 and the *y* number is +2.

Sample Student Response 3

Probe Item. c. No. Those numbers are too big to be right. The line is gradual.

Sample Student Response 4

Probe Item. b. Yes. The −6*x* means the line starts to the left of the *y* line and it does.

Is It a Linear Function?

4.5

Determine whether each of the following represents a linear function.

Circle the correct answer.	Explain your choice.
1. $$y = -\frac{3}{5}x + 2$$ a. Yes b. No c. Not enough information	
2. $$y = x(x + 5)$$ a. Yes b. No c. Not enough information	
3. <table><tr><td>Input</td><td>Output</td></tr><tr><td>−3</td><td>13</td></tr><tr><td>−2</td><td>10</td></tr><tr><td>1</td><td>1</td></tr><tr><td>2</td><td>−2</td></tr><tr><td>3</td><td>−5</td></tr></table>a. Yes b. No c. Not enough information	
4. <table><tr><td>Input</td><td>Output</td></tr><tr><td>−3</td><td>9</td></tr><tr><td>−2</td><td>4</td></tr><tr><td>−1</td><td>1</td></tr><tr><td>2</td><td>4</td></tr><tr><td>3</td><td>9</td></tr></table>a. Yes b. No c. Not enough information	

Teacher Notes: Is It a Linear Function?

Questions to Consider About the Key Mathematical Concepts

When solving problems involving equations and tables, can students interpret key features to determine whether they represent a linear function? To what extent do they

- make sense of information given in equation and table form?
- model how to recognize linear and nonlinear relationships when given an equation or table of values?
- describe key features of linear functions in symbolic or tabular form?

Common Core Connection (CCSS.Math.Content.8.F.A.3; CCSS.Math.Content.8.F.B.4)

Grade: Eighth

Domain: Functions

Cluster:

Define, evaluate, and compare functions.

3. Interpret the equation $y = mx + b$ as defining a linear function whose graph is a straight line; give examples of functions that are not linear. For example, the function $A = s^2$ giving the area of a square as a function of its side length is not linear because its graph contains the points (1,1), (2,4), and (3,9), which are not on a straight line.

Use functions to model relationships between quantities.

4. Construct a function to model a linear relationship between two quantities. Determine the rate of change and initial value of the function from a description of a relationship or from two (x, y) values, including reading these from a table or from a graph. Interpret the rate of change and initial value of a linear function in terms of the situation it models, and in terms of its graph or a table of values.

Uncovering Student Understanding About the Key Concepts

Using the Is It a Linear Function? Probe can provide the following information about how the students are thinking about multiple representations of linear functions.

Do they		*Do they*
• recognize key features of linear equations when written in various forms?	OR	• guess at which equations are linear?
• understand that input values (*x*) in the table need to vary directly to the output values (*y*) for it to represent a linear relationship?	OR	• see the table as numbers that cannot be compared?
• see various representations as valid ways to depict a linear relationship?	OR	• only see either equations or tables as valid ways to represent a linear function?

Exploring Excerpts From Educational Resources and Related Research

Common areas of difficulty for students:

Students fail to recognize the underlying equivalence when the same set of points is represented by a graph or an equation or a table. They tend to see changes in form as producing unrelated representations. (NCTM, 1999, p. 215)

Students may not see the links between different representations of a functional relation—for example, the mutual dependence between a function's graph and equation, or between its table and equation. (Driscoll, 1999, p. 146)

Students do not understand non-linear relationships such as squaring and square rooting. (Stepans et al., 2005, p. 150)

Surveying the Prompts and Selected Responses in the Probe

The Probe consists of four separate selected response items. The prompts and selected responses are designed to elicit understandings and common difficulties as described below:

If a student chooses	*It is likely that the student*
1a, 2b (correct answers)	• understands the characteristics of a linear function in equation form [See Sample Student Response 1]. *Look for indication of the student's understanding in the written explanations of how the student got the answer.*

If a student chooses	It is likely that the student
3a, 4b (correct answers)	• uses information given in a table to find relevant information about the relationship between the variables to determine a linear or nonlinear function [See Sample Student Response 1].
Any other response	• does not have a conceptual understanding of a linear function. The student probably does not recognize the characteristics of a linear equation or the relationship between variables [See Sample Student Responses 2, 3, 4, and 5].

Teaching Implications and Considerations

Ideas for eliciting more information from students about their understanding and difficulties:

- What do you know about a linear function?
- What are some key features of the equations that might help us determine whether they are linear?
- What should the power of x be in a linear equation? What do the numbers tell you in the equation?
- How can you use the numbers in the tables to determine if there is a linear relationship?
- Can you graph the numbers in the table to get an idea of what the graph looks like?

Ideas for planning instruction in response to what you learned from the results of administering the Probe:

- Allow students ample opportunities to explore linear and nonlinear functions in which they use tables, graphs, words, and symbolic representations.
- Have students explore the relationship between the variables with each of the different types of representation.
- Use technology as an avenue for students to make connections between the different types of representations.
- Help students look for relevant information in equations and tables that help to determine the type of relationship they represent.

Sample Student Responses to Is It a Linear Function?

Responses That Suggest Understanding

Sample Student Response 1

Probe Item 1. a. It is a linear function because it is written in slope-intercept form with the slope in front of the x and the y-intercept behind the x. Also there is only one x.

Probe Item 2. b. There are 2 x's which would make the equation x^2 which is not linear.

Probe Item 3. a. This is a linear function because the y's go down at the same rate, although it doesn't look like it because the table doesn't show −1 or 0.

Probe Item 4. b. It is not linear because at the beginning as x's go up, y's go down until you get to $x = 2$, then the y's start to go up.

Responses That Suggest Difficulty

Sample Student Response 2

Probe Item 1. c. We don't know what x or y is.

Probe Item 2. c. We don't know what x or y is.

Probe Item 3. b. The y's don't go down the same each time.

Sample Student Response 3

Probe Item 1. a. It has no repeats.

Probe Item 2. c. We don't know what x is.

Probe Item 4. a. The x's don't repeat.

Sample Student Response 4

Probe Item 3. b. The x's don't multiply by anything to get y's.

Probe Item 4. a. The x's multiply by themselves to get the y's.

Sample Student Response 5

Probe Item 3. b. It is not an equation.

Probe Item 4. b. It is not an equation.

Sample Student Response 6

Probe Item 2. a. There is no exponent so it is linear.

5

Statistics and Probability Probes

The content of the Probes in this chapter aligns with the standards for Grades 6 through 8. The Probes will also be relevant beyond the aligned grade level for students in higher grades who have not yet met standards from previous grade levels as well as for students who have already met the standards at their own grade level.

We developed these Probes to address this critical area of focus for middle school students, described in the standards (CCSSO, 2010) as follows:

- Develop understanding of statistical variability.
- Summarize and describe distributions.
- Use random sampling to draw inferences about a population.
- Draw informal comparative inferences about two populations.
- Investigate chance processes and develop, use, and evaluate probability models.
- Investigate patterns of association in bivariate data.

> The content of the Probes in this chapter aligns with the standards for Grades 6 through 8. The Probes will also be relevant beyond the aligned grade level for students in higher grades who have not yet met standards from previous grade levels as well as for students who have already met the standards at their own grade level.

Common Core Math Content

Common Core Mathematical Content	Related Question	Probe Name
Recognize that a measure of center for a numerical data set summarizes all of its values with a single number, while a measure of variation describes how its values vary with a single number. CCSS.Math.Content.6.SP.A.3	When solving problems involving measures of center and spread, can students use mean, median, and mode measures to analyze data?	Measures of Center and Spread (p. 121)
Find probabilities of compound events using organized lists, tables, tree diagrams, and simulation. CCSS.Math.Content.7.SP.C.8	When solving problems involving chance, can students apply their understanding about simple and compound probability of independent events?	What's the Chance? (p. 126)
Construct and interpret scatter plots for bivariate measurement data to investigate patterns of association between two quantities. Describe patterns such as clustering, outliers, positive or negative association, linear association, and nonlinear association. CCSS.Math.Content.8.SP.A.1	When solving problems involving scatterplots, can students describe associations between quantities in terms of positive, negative, or no correlation?	Scatterplots (p. 131)

Measures of Center and Spread

Mr. Hernandez collected the following information about students' scores on test that consisted of a total of 100 points:

The median is 84 points.
The mode is 90 points.
The mean is 88 points.

Decide whether the statement is True or False.	Explain your choice.
1. **More students scored 90 points than any other number of points.** a. True b. False c. Not enough information	
2. **At least half the students scored 88 or fewer points.** a. True b. False c. Not enough information	
3. **The scores range from 84 to 90.** a. True b. False c. Not enough information	

Teacher Notes: Measures of Center and Spread

Questions to Consider About the Key Mathematical Concepts

When solving problems involving measures of center and spread, can students use mean, median, and mode measures to analyze data? To what extent do they

- make sense of information given about a data set using measures of center?
- describe what the measures of center tell us about a data set and how the information can be used to infer characteristic of the data set?

Common Core Connection (CCSS.Math.Content.6.SP.A.3; CCSS.Math.Content.6.SP.B.5)

Grade: Sixth

Domain: Statistics and Probability

Cluster:

Develop understanding of statistical variability.

3. Recognize that a measure of center for a numerical data set summarizes all of its values with a single number, while a measure of variation describes how its values vary with a single number.

Summarize and describe distributions.

5. Summarize numerical data sets in relation to their context, such as by

    5a. reporting the number of observations;
    5b. describing the nature of the attribute under investigation, including how it was measured and its units of measurement;
    5c. giving quantitative measures of center (median and/or mean) and variability (interquartile range and/or mean absolute deviation), as well as describing any overall pattern and any striking deviations from the overall pattern with reference to the context in which the data were gathered; or
    5d. relating the choice of measures of center and variability to the shape of the data distribution and the context in which the data were gathered.

Uncovering Student Understanding About the Key Concepts

Using the Measures of Center and Spread Probe can provide the following information about how students are thinking about mean, median, and mode.

Do they		*Do they*
• have meaningful understanding of mean, median, and mode?	OR	• see them as procedures one can use when given a data set?
• understand how measures of center represent a set of data?	OR	• see them as arbitrary numbers?
• understand that the measures of spread are related to but different from measures of center, and one can reason about possible ranges from given averages?	OR	• see the measures of center as giving specific information about the range of the data set or that nothing can be assumed about the range?

Exploring Excerpts From Educational Resources and Related Research

Common areas of difficulty for students:

While many students can find the mean of a data set, they have difficulty understanding what the mean tells us (or doesn't tell) about the data set. They also have trouble distinguishing among mean, median, and mode in terms of what each tells about the data set. (Stepans et al., 2005, p. 192)

[They] do not know how to choose between the mean, median, and mode as an appropriate measure of central tendency in a given situation. (Stepans et al., 2005, p. 190)

Students often treat [data given to them] as numbers without context, making it difficult to reason from the data. (Stepans et al., 2005, p. 191)

Research involving students from middle school through college suggests that few students know much more about means than how to compute them (Cai, 1998; Pollatski, Lima, & Well, 1987). Thus, even children who can compute the mean often do not understand why the computation works or what the result represents. Although the add-and-divide algorithm is relatively simple to execute, developing a conceptual underpinning that allows one to use the mean sensibly is surprisingly difficult. (NCTM, 2003, p. 204)

Computational facility with average does not guarantee that conceptual understanding or contextual connections about average will follow in our students. (NCTM, 2007, Research Brief)

Surveying the Prompts and Selected Responses in the Probe

The Probe consists of three selected responses items. The prompts and selected responses are designed to elicit understandings and common difficulties as described below:

If a student chooses	It is likely that the student
1a, 2b, 3b (correct answers)	• understands the different measures of center and can reason about characteristics of the actual data set based on the measures given [See Sample Student Response 1]. *Look for indication of the student's understanding in the written explanations of how the student got the answer.*
Any other answers	• does not have a clear understanding of what information each measure of center is providing and what information can (or cannot) be reasoned about the data set from the measures [See Sample Student Responses 2, 3, and 4].

Teaching Implications and Considerations

Ideas for eliciting more information from students about their understanding and difficulties:

- What is an average? Which of the words (mean, median, or mode) did you describe?
- What does each of the measures tell us about the data set?
- Does the mean have to be a member of the data set? The median? The mode?
- Is there any information given specifically about the range of the data?
- What measure(s) of center might help you to better understand the range? (Students should be able to reason that if the median is 84 and that there are values above and below, based on the given mean and mode, there need to be values below 84.)
- How are the measures of center related/similar? How are they different?

Ideas for planning instruction in response to what you learned from the results of administering the Probe:

- Emphasize that measures of center do not describe everything about a set of data but they can provide a snapshot of the data.
- Explore measures of center and spread in meaningful contexts.
- Allow students to ask their own questions, collect their own data based on their questions, display the collected data in an appropriate way, and present their findings to their peers.
- Rather than providing students data and having them compute the measures of center, provide them with the measures of center and have them construct data sets that will produce the measures given.
- Students should explore the concept of mean only after they have a strong foundational understanding of median and mode. (Stepans et al., 2005, p. 192)
- Provide opportunities for students to understand that the mean is a "balancing" point where the data points are evenly distributed above and below this point.

Sample Student Responses to Measures of Center and Spread

Responses That Suggest Understanding

Sample Student Response 1

Probe Item 1. True. The mode is 90, which tells us that score showed up the most.

Probe Item 2. False. The mean is 88 not the median. The mean is all of the data added together and divided by how many data there are. It doesn't tell us about how many are above it or below.

Probe Item 3. False. If the median is 84 then this is the middle score. There are scores above it and below it so the range can't be starting at 84. Plus just because the mode is at 90 doesn't mean it is the highest score.

Responses That Suggest Difficulty

Sample Student Response 2

Probe Item 2. True. The mean is the average so there are the same number above as below.

Sample Student Response 3

Probe Item 3. True. This must be true because they are the lowest and highest scores given.

Sample Student Response 4

Probe Item 3. There is not enough information to tell the range.

What's the Chance?

Two jars have black and white gumballs.

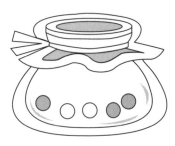

| Jar A | Jar B |

If a gumball is chosen from each jar without looking, determine whether each statement is true or false.

True or False?	Explain your choice.
1. **There is a better chance of getting a black gumball from Jar A.** True False	
2. **The probability of getting a white gumball from both jars is $\frac{4}{25}$.** True False	
3. **The probability of getting a black gumball from both jars is $\frac{9}{15}$.** True False	

Source: Adapted from Rose Tobey and Minton (2011).

Teacher Notes: What's the Chance?

Questions to Consider About the Key Mathematical Concepts

When solving problems involving chance, can students apply their understanding about simple and compound probability of independent events? To what extent do they

- make sense of the problem using multiplicative reasoning?
- make comparisons using relative size?
- model the outcomes using an organized list, table, or tree diagram?

**Common Core Connection
(CCSS.Math.Content.7.SP.C.8)**

Grade: Seventh

Domain: Statistics and Probability

Cluster:

Investigate chance processes and develop, use, and evaluate probability models.

8. Find probabilities of compound events using organized lists, tables, tree diagrams, and simulation.

Uncovering Student Understanding About the Key Concepts

Using the What's the Chance? Probe can provide the following information about how the students are thinking about probability concepts.

Do they

- apply multiplicative reasoning when determining probability (focus on relative difference)?

OR

- determine the probability by noticing the number of possible occurrences of the wanted outcome divided by the number of all possible outcomes?

Do they

- apply additive reasoning by counting, combining, and/or finding the difference (focus on absolute difference)?

OR

- determine the probability as the number of possible occurrences of the wanted outcome divided by the remaining possible occurrences?

Do they

- treat each jar separately when determining the probability?

OR

Do they

- combine the numbers as if finding simple probability?

Exploring Excerpts From Educational Resources and Related Research

Common areas of difficulty for students:

[Jones, Langrall, Thorton, and Mogill] theorized that children exhibit four levels of thinking about probability situations: subjective, transitional, informal quantitative, and numerical. (NCTM, 2003, p. 217)

Students might not possess a process model for chance experiments, because they do not envision the results of a single trial of an experiment as just one of many possible outcomes that will vary across a sample space if the experiment is repeated. (NCTM, 2003, p. 218)

Data from the Mathematics Assessment for Learning and Teaching (MaLT) project data base indicate that students demonstrate the following types of difficulties with related probability tasks: believing the sample should reflect the population from which it's drawn; all chances of equally likely; . . . and estimating chances based on easily accessible memories of events and their frequencies. (Ryan & Williams, 2007, pp. 130–131)

Surveying the Prompts and Selected Responses in the Probe

The Probe consists of three related true/false items. The prompts and selected responses are designed to elicit understandings and common difficulties as described below:

If a student chooses	*It is likely that the student*
1 False; 2 True; 3 False (correct answers)	- is correctly applying concepts including comparing relative size and finding probabilities involving compound events. - in problem 1 is using doubling, ratios, and/or percents to determine the chance is equally likely. - in problems 2 and 3 is correctly describing the possible outcomes though lists, tables, or tree diagrams [See Sample Student Responses 1 and 2]. *Look for indication of the student's understanding in the written explanations of how the student got the answer.*

If a student chooses	It is likely that the student
1 True	• is using an absolute comparison of "there are more black gumballs in Jar B than in Jar A" [See Sample Student Response 3].
2 False	• is calculating the probability by combining the gumballs and treating it as a simple event: total of 6 white gumballs and 15 gumballs total [See Sample Student Response 4].
3 True	• is calculating the probability by combining the gumballs and treating as a simple event: total of 9 black gumballs and 15 gumballs total [See Sample Student Response 5].

Teaching Implications and Considerations

Ideas for eliciting more information from students about their understanding and difficulties:

- Can you explain to me what it means to pick a gumball from both jars?
- How could you describe the relationship between the number of black gumballs and the total number of gumballs in each bag?

Ideas for planning instruction in response to what you learned from the results of administering the Probe:

- Students should learn about probability as a measurement of the likelihood of events.
- Students should explore probability through experiments that have only a few outcomes.
- Computer simulations provide a quick method of collecting large samples in providing experimental data that are close to the theoretical probability.
- To correct misconceptions, it is helpful for students to make predictions and then compare the predictions with actual outcomes.
- Students should encounter the idea that although they can't determine outcomes, they can predict the frequency of various outcomes.
- A solid understanding of ratio and proportion is critical for understanding relative frequency.

Sample Student Responses to What's the Chance?

Responses That Suggest Understanding

Sample Student Response 1

Probe Item 1. Both jars have the same chance of getting a black gumball because each jar has the same ratio of white to black gumballs. Jar B just has twice as many of each.

Probe Item 2. Jar A is $\frac{2}{5}$ and Jar B is $\frac{2}{5}$. To find probability of both, multiply and get $\frac{4}{25}$.

Sample Student Response 2

Probe Item 1. Jar A has 3 black ones out of 5 total, Jar B has 6 black ones out of 10 total so there is the same chance to get a black one.

Probe Item 2. I numbered the gumballs and started to make a list of everything that could happen if you take a gumball from each. I figured out there would be 50 different ways and 8 of those ways were 2 white gumballs. $\frac{8}{50}$ is same as $\frac{4}{25}$.

Responses That Suggest Difficulty

Sample Student Response 3

Probe Item 1. I think this is false because there are a lot more black gumballs in Jar B so of course you will have a greater chance to get one out of Jar B.

Sample Student Response 4

Probe Item 2. This is true because there are not 4 white out of 25 total. There are 6 white and 15 total.

Sample Student Response 5

Probe Item 3. This is true because there are a total of 9 black gumballs and 15 gumballs all together.

Scatterplots

Determine whether the data in each scatterplot shows a positive, negative, or no correlation or whether there isn't enough information to determine the correlation.

Circle the correct answer.	Explain your choice.
1. a. Positive b. Negative c. No correlation d. Not enough information	
2. a. Positive b. Negative c. No correlation d. Not enough information	
3. a. Positive b. Negative c. No correlation d. Not enough information	

Teacher Notes: Scatterplots

Questions to Consider About the Key Mathematical Concepts

When solving problems involving scatterplots, can students describe associations between quantities in term of positive, negative, or no correlation? To what extent do they

- make sense of the association between two quantities in terms of correlation (or no correlation)?
- recognize the relationship between two quantities with linear trends as having positive or negative correlation?

Common Core Connection (CCSS.Math.Content.8.SP.A.1)

Grade: Eighth

Domain: Statistics and Probability

Cluster:

Investigate patterns of association in bivariate data.

1. Construct and interpret scatter plots for bivariate measurement data to investigate patterns of association between two quantities. Describe patterns such as clustering, outliers, positive or negative association, linear association, and nonlinear association.

Uncovering Student Understanding About the Key Concepts

Using the Scatterplots Probe can provide the following information about how the students are thinking about association between two quantities.

Do they

- determine whether two quantities show correlation by thinking about the linear (or nonlinear) trend of the data?

- distinguish between positive, negative, or no correlation?

Do they

OR • focus on the quadrant(s) the data reside in?

OR • use positive correlation in conjunction with how "linear" the data appear to be?

Exploring Excerpts From Educational Resources and Related Research

Common areas of difficulty for students:

Data from the Mathematics Assessment for Learning and Teaching (MaLT) project data base indicate that students demonstrate the following types of difficulties with correlation: identifies negative correlation with no correlation and that data is either correlated or not correlated. (Ryan & Williams, 2007, p. 221)

Surveying the Prompts and Selected Responses in the Probe

The Probe consists of three separate selected response items. The prompts and selected responses are designed to elicit understandings and common difficulties as described below:

If a student chooses	It is likely that the student
1a, 2c, 3b (correct answers)	• recognizes correlation as a linear relationship between quantities [See Sample Student Response 1]. *Look for indication of the student's understanding in the written explanations of how the student got the answer.*
1b, 2a	• is confusing correlation with quadrants [See Sample Student Responses 2 and 4].
3c	• recognizes the linear trend in the data but does not consider the trend as negative correlation. • associates negative correlation with no correlation [See Sample Student Responses 3 and 5].
2b	• is confusing no correlation with negative correlation.
1d, 2d, 3d	• believes additional information is needed about the context or actual data values to determine correlation [See Sample Student Responses 2 and 5].
Miscellaneous other answers	• may associate correlation with only first quadrant. • has no understanding of correlation so is applying erroneous thinking.

Teaching Implications and Considerations

Ideas for eliciting more information from students about their understanding and difficulties:

- Can you draw a line of best fit for this data? How could this help you think about correlation?
- Does the line you have drawn (if one can be drawn) have a positive or negative slope (rate of change)? How do you know?
- Does slope (rate of change) relate to correlation? How?

Ideas for planning instruction in response to what you learned from the results of administering the Probe:

- Begin by having students create scatterplots from data they have collected.
- Have students analyze scatterplots for clusters and gaps and "for overall trends overall positive or negative trend in the cloud of points, a linear or nonlinear (curved) pattern, and a strong or weak association between the two variables, using these terms in describing the nature of the observed association between the variables" (Common Core Standards Writing Team, 2011c, p. 11).
- Connect strong and weak linear associations between two quantities with equations of lines of best fit. Use technology tools that allow students to compare their line to a calculated line of best fit.
- Provide experiences with bivariant data with linear trends as well as other trends that are nonlinear.
- Have discussions on why the quadrant location of the data does not decide whether a linear trend has positive, negative, or no correlation.

Sample Student Responses to Scatterplots

Responses That Suggest Understanding

Sample Student Response 1

Probe Item 1. a. If you look at the graph carefully it shows the data going up. This would make it positive correlation.

Probe Item 2. c. The data points on this graph have no pattern that show them growing or decreasing at a constant rate. They are too scattered.

Probe Item 3. b. The data points are decreasing at a constant rate.

Responses That Suggest Difficulty

Sample Student Response 2

Probe Item 1. c. There is no correlation because it is positive on the *x* axis and negative on the *y* axis.

Probe Item 2. a. This is a positive correlation because all of the points are in the positive part of the graph (*x* and *y*).

Probe Item 3. d. Not enough information because it is positive and negative on x and y.

Sample Student Response 3

Probe Item 3. a. The points on this one are in a straight line so would have positive correlation.

Sample Student Response 4

Probe Item 1. b. This is negative because the points are in the negative quadrant (below the line).

Probe Item 3. d. There is not enough information because the points are in three different quadrants.

Sample Student Response 5

Probe Item 1. c. There is no correlation because the points are too clustered.

Probe Item 3. c. The points are making a line but it is going downward so there is not a correlation.

6

Geometry Probes

The content of the Probes in this chapter aligns with the standards for Grades 6 through 8. The Probes and their variations will also be relevant beyond the aligned grade level for students in higher grades who have not yet met standards from previous grade levels as well as for students who have already met the standards at their own grade level.

We developed these Probes to address this critical area of focus for middle school students, described in the standards (CCSSO, 2010) as follows:

- Solve real-world and mathematical problems involving area, surface area, and volume.
- Draw, construct, and describe geometrical figures and describe the relationships between them.
- Solve real-life and mathematical problems involving angle measure, area, surface area, and volume.
- Understand congruence and similarity using physical models, transparencies, or geometry software.
  - Understand and apply the Pythagorean Theorem.
  - Solve real-world and mathematical problems involving volume of cylinders, cones, and spheres.

The content of the Probes in this chapter aligns with the standards for Grades 6 through 8. The Probes and their variations will also be relevant beyond the aligned grade level for students in higher grades who have not yet met standards from previous grade levels as well as for students who have already met the standards at their own grade level.

Take a look at the variations that are available with some of the Probes in this chapter. All of these variations address geometry but may extend the idea or offer a different structure for administering them. When available, variation Probes follow the Teacher Notes and associated reproducibles for the related original Probe.

Common Core Math Content

Common Core Mathematical Content	Related Question	Probe Name
Find the area of right triangles, other triangles, special quadrilaterals, and polygons by composing into rectangles or decomposing into triangles and other shapes. CCSS.Math.Content.6.G.A.1	When solving problems involving perimeter and area, do students understand that perimeter and area are not dependent on each other?	Perimeter and Area (p. 138)
Use facts about supplementary, complementary, vertical, and adjacent angles in a multi-step problem to write and solve simple equations for an unknown angle in a figure. CCSS.Math.Content.7.G.B.5	When solving problems involving relationships between interior and exterior angles of a triangle, can students use characteristics and properties to compare angle measures?	Properties of Angles (p. 143)
Solve real-world and mathematical problems involving area, volume and surface area of two- and three-dimensional objects composed of triangles, quadrilaterals, polygons, cubes, and right prisms. CCSS.Math.Content.7.G.B.6	When solving problems involving geometric measurement, can students determine the volume of a prism given either side lengths or area of a base and the height?	Finding Volume (p. 148) Variation: Volume of the Box (p. 153)
Solve problems involving scale drawings of geometric figures, including computing actual lengths and areas from a scale drawing and reproducing a scale drawing at a different scale. CCSS.Math.Content.7.G.A.1	When solving problems involving scale drawings, can students use concepts of similarity and proportional reasoning to find a missing side length?	Scale (p. 154)
Apply the Pythagorean Theorem to determine unknown side lengths in right triangles in real-world and mathematical problems in two and three dimensions. CCSS.Math.Content.8.G.B.7	When solving problems involving triangles, can students correctly use the Pythagorean Theorem converse to determine which are right triangles?	Right Triangles (p. 159)
Know the formulas for the volumes of cones, cylinders, and spheres and use them to solve real-world and mathematical problems. CCSS.Math.Content.8.G.C.9	When solving problems involving three-dimensional figures, can students determine how to find the height of the figure?	Heights of Solids (p. 164)
Draw (freehand, with ruler and protractor, and with technology) geometric shapes with given conditions. CCSS.Math.Content.7.G.A.2	When solving problems involving geometric shapes, can students recognize parallelograms?	Parallelograms (p. 169) Variation: Is It a Parallelogram? (p. 174)

Perimeter and Area

The two rectangles have the same perimeter.

Rectangle A:
    Length = a inches
    Width = b inches
    Perimeter = 40 inches

Rectangle B:
    Length= d inches
    Width = e inches
    Perimeter = 40 inches

Decide if you agree or disagree with each student's statement about the rectangles.

Statement	Explain your choice:
1. *The two rectangles could have different side measures.* **Circle one:** Agree Disagree	
2. *The two rectangles have equivelent area measures.* **Circle one:** Agree Disagree	

Teacher Notes: Perimeter and Area

Questions to Consider About the Key Mathematical Concepts

When solving problems involving perimeter and area, do students understand that perimeter and area are not dependent on each other? To what extent do they

- make sense of figures with the same perimeter but different areas?
- reason about whether figures with different dimensions can have the same perimeter but different areas?
- show mathematically that two rectangles having the same perimeter do not necessarily have the same dimensions or area?

Common Core Connection (CCSS.Math.Content.6.G.A.1)

Grade: Sixth

Domain: Geometry

Cluster:

Solve real-world and mathematical problems involving area, surface area, and volume.

1. Find the area of right triangles, other triangles, special quadrilaterals, and polygons by composing into rectangles or decomposing into triangles and other shapes; apply these techniques in the context of solving real-world and mathematical problems.

Uncovering Student Understanding About the Key Concepts

Using the Perimeter and Area Probe can provide the following information about how the students are thinking about perimeter and area being related to a figure's side lengths.

Do they
- understand that two figures can have the same perimeter but have different dimensions?

OR

Do they
- think that figures with the same perimeter must have the same dimensions?

- reason that figures with the same perimeter can have different areas?

OR

- see area as being dependent on perimeter?

Do they

- have a conceptual understanding of perimeter and area?

OR

Do they

- know perimeter and area as formulas with calculation procedures to follow?

Exploring Excerpts From Educational Resources and Related Research

Common areas of difficulty for students:

Many students believe that as perimeter remains constant, the area will remain constant as well. (Stepans et al., 2005, p. 234)

[Area and perimeter are continually a source of confusion for students.] Perhaps it is because both involve regions to be measured or because students are taught formulas for both concepts and tend to get the formulas confused. (Van de Walle, 2007, p. 386)

By the time that students enter the middle grades, most of them are between the concrete and informal deduction levels defined by the van Hieles. In geometry, students should have a concept of what area and perimeter are and be able to describe their attributes. They should be able to derive the formulas for area and perimeter of some geometric shapes, such as rectangles, squares, and triangles, and use those formulas to find area and perimeter. Although many middle-grades students can solve these problems, they may not have fully conceptualized the meanings of the words. They become confused by the formulas and find area when they are asked for perimeter and perimeter when they are asked for area. (Malloy, 1999, p. 88)

Adolescents bring to the classroom varied conceptions of measurement, which may be in the form of basic applications or general formulas. All too often, a fundamental understanding of these ideas is sacrificed while students learn general formulas. This situation is particularly true for attributes of perimeter and area. (Chappell & Thompson, 1999, p. 20)

Surveying the Prompts and Selected Responses in the Probe

The Probe consists of two selected response items related to a common set of measures. The prompts and selected responses are designed to elicit understandings and common difficulties as described in the following table:

If a student chooses	It is likely that the student
1 Agree 2 Disagree (correct answers)	• understands that there are many different-sized rectangles that could have a perimeter of 40. The student also likely understands that perimeter and area are not dependent on each other and that figures with the same perimeter can have different areas [See Sample Student Response 1]. *Look for indication of the student's understanding in the written explanations of how the student got the answer.*
1 Disagree 2 Agree	• does not have a solid conceptual understanding of perimeter and area or does not understand the formulas completely. These students often understand equivalent perimeters as meaning congruent shapes [See Sample Student Responses 2 and 3].

Teaching Implications and Considerations

Ideas for eliciting more information from students about their understanding and difficulties:

- What is the perimeter of a figure? How do you find perimeter?
- What are some side length dimensions that would give a perimeter of 40? Can you think of some different dimensions that would also give 40?
- What is the area of a figure? How do you find area?
- What rectangular measurements would give an area of 40? Are there any other measurements that would give an area of 40?
- What is the difference between perimeter and area?

Ideas for planning instruction in response to what you learned from the results of administering the Probe:

- Students should have frequent opportunities with hands-on activities, including the use of technology, to measure and compare perimeter and area of differently shaped objects.
- Have students develop formulas for perimeter, area, and volume of different objects on their own through inquiry to help them have a deeper conceptual understanding of what the formulas mean.
- Composing and decomposing shapes should be used as a method of finding perimeter and areas of various objects and comparing how changing one dimension affects perimeter and area.

Sample Student Responses to Perimeter and Area

Responses That Suggest Understanding

Sample Student Response 1

Probe Item 1. Agree. Rectangle 1 could have length = 15 in. and width = 5 in. to have a perimeter of 40. Rectangle B could have the length = 18 in. and the width = 2 in., which would also have a perimeter of 40 in.

Probe Item 2. Disagree. For the above side lengths the areas would not be the same. One would be 75 in^2 and the other would be 36 in^2.

Responses That Suggest Difficulty

Sample Student Response 2

Probe Item 1. Disagree. The two rectangles would have to have the same dimensions to have the same perimeter.

Probe Item 2. Agree. They would also have the same area.

Sample Student Response 3

Probe Item 2. Agree. The two rectangles could have different side measures but if their perimeters are the same then their areas would also be the same.

Properties of Angles

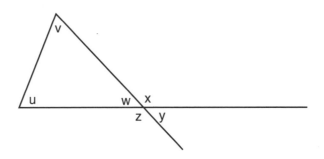

Use the above figure to determine if the statement is true or false.

Circle the correct answer.	Explain your choice.
1. $m \angle w < m \angle y$ a. True b. False c. Not enough information	
2. $m \angle x + m \angle y = 180°$ a. True b. False c. Not enough information	
3. $m \angle u + m \angle v = m \angle x$ a. True b. False c. Not enough information	
4. $m \angle x + m \angle u > 180°$ a. True b. False c. Not enough information	

Teacher Notes: Properties of Angles

Questions to Consider About the Key Mathematical Concepts

When solving problems involving relationships between interior and exterior angles of a triangle, can students use characteristics and properties to compare angle measures? To what extent do they

- make sense of the relationships between interior and exterior angles of a triangle and use the properties of triangles and angles to compare angle measures?
- use geometric reasoning to compare measures of angles, given statements about a figure?
- describe how characteristics and properties of angles and triangles are used to reason about the truth of a given statement?

Common Core Connection (CCSS.Math.Content.7.G.B.5)

Grade: Seventh

Domain: Geometry

Cluster:

Solve real-life and mathematical problems involving angle measure, area, surface area, and volume.

5. Use facts about supplementary, complementary, vertical, and adjacent angles in a multistep problem to write and solve simple equations for an unknown angle in a figure.

Common Core Connection (CCSS.Math.Content.8.G.A.5)

Grade: Eighth

Domain: Geometry

Cluster:

Understand congruence and similarity using physical models, transparencies, or geometry software.

5. Use informal arguments to establish facts about the angle sum and exterior angle of triangles, about the angles created when parallel lines are cut by a transversal, and the angle-angle criterion for similarity of triangles. For example, arrange three copies of the same triangle so that the sum of the three angles appears to form a line, and give an argument in terms of transversals why this is so.

Uncovering Student Understanding About the Key Concepts

Using the Properties of Angles Probe can provide the following information about how the students are thinking about angle relationships.

Do they

- recognize congruent and supplementary relationships of angles based on properties?

OR

- use logical reasoning to analyze angle relationships?

Do they

OR

- use intuitive rules to incorrectly assume congruency?

OR

- use inappropriate mental images about angles of a triangle?

Exploring Excerpts From Educational Resources and Related Research

Common areas of difficulty for students:

School geometry that is presented in an axiomatic fashion assumes that students think on a formal deductive level. However, that is usually not the case, and they lack prerequisite understandings about geometry. This lack creates a gap between their level of thinking and that required for the geometry that they are expected to learn. (van Heile, 1999, p. 310)

[Although students can logically organize ideas at van Hiele's Level 3], "they still do not grasp that logical deduction is the method for establishing geometric truths." (NCTM, 2003, p. 153)

Students refer to geometric properties and motions in their justifications, although they are not always accurate. Much remains for students to learn about congruence. (NCTM, 2003 p. 161)

When people think they do not always use definitions of concepts, but rather, concept images—a combination of all the mental pictures and properties that have been associated with the concept (Vinner & Hershkowitz, 1980). Students who not only know a correct verbal description of a concept but also have strongly associated a specific visual image, or concept image, with the concept may have difficulty applying the verbal description correctly. (NCTM, 2003, p. 163)

Surveying the Prompts and Selected Responses in the Probe

The Probe consists of four selected response items, each related to a common figure. The prompts and selected responses are designed to elicit understandings and common difficulties as described in the following table:

If a student chooses	It is likely that the student
1b, 2a, 3a, 4c (correct answers)	• reasons correctly about the relationships of angles in a triangle. The student has an understanding of linear pairs, vertical angles, sum of interior angles, and properties of exterior angles [See Sample Student Responses 1, 2, and 3]. *Look for indication of the student's understanding in the written explanations of how the student got the answer.*
1a, 4a, 4b	• uses intuitive rules based on what the angle measures look like. The student's answer is based on a perception of the measures instead of what is actually known [See Sample Student Responses 4, 5, and 6].
1c, 2b, 2c, 3b, 3c	• does not recognize the linear pair or reasons the angles are supplementary (add to 180°). The student also might not understand the properties of exterior angle measures being equal to the sum of the remote interior angles [See Sample Student Responses 4, 5, and 6].

Teaching Implications and Considerations

Ideas for eliciting more information from students about their understanding and difficulties:

- What different types of angles can be seen in the figure?
- What are the properties of those angles?
- Which properties of triangles are about angles?
- Can you use any of the properties about triangles to compare the angles?

Ideas for planning instruction in response to what you learned from the results of administering the Probe:

- Use a variety of mental imagery and kinesthetic opportunities to build understanding of geometric concepts.
- Provide practice with multiple examples of varying angle orientations and ray lengths to allow students different visual experiences.
- Allow students to progress through van Hiele's first three levels of geometric thinking. The levels are Level 1 Visual, Level 2 Descriptive/ Analytic, and Level 3 Abstract/Relational.
- Include practice and discussion of logical reasoning and justification as part of students' daily geometric learning.

Sample Student Responses to Properties of Angles

Responses That Suggest Understanding

Sample Student Response 1

Probe Item 1. b (False). Angles *w* and *y* are the same measure as they are vertical angles.

Probe Item 2. a (True). Angles *x* and *y* are a linear pair so they equal 180°.

Probe Item 3. a (True). I think this is true because angles $w + x = 180$ and angles *u*, *v*, and *w* = 180. This would mean that $x = u + v$.

Probe Item 4. c (Not enough information). I am not sure about this one. I think I might need more information.

Sample Student Response 2

Probe Item 2. a (True). *x* and *y* form a flat line so it is 180.

Sample Student Response 3

Probe Item 3. a (True). This would be true because angles *v* and *u* are remote interior angles and they equal angle *x*.

Responses That Suggest Difficulty

Sample Student Response 4

Probe Item 1. b (False). Angle *y* actually looks bigger than *w* so I don't think this is true.

Probe Item 3. c (Not Enough Information). That would be an estimation so I don't think there is enough information.

Sample Student Response 5

Probe Item 1. a (True). I see that they are the same.

Sample Student Response 6

Probe Item 4. a (True). *x* and *u* form a flat line so they equal 180.

Finding Volume

Determine the volume of the figure.	Explain your choice.
1. 4 m 6 m 10 m a. 20 m³ b. 240 m³ c. Not enough information	
2. 24 cm² 4 cm a. 28 cm³ b. 96 cm³ c. Not enough information	
3. 10 m 6 m 8 m a. 480 m³ b. 240 m³ c. Not enough information	
4. 40 m² 7 m a. 280 m³ b. 140 m³ c. Not enough information	

Teacher Notes: Finding Volume

Questions to Consider About the Key Mathematical Concepts

When solving problems involving geometric measurement, can students determine the volume of a prism given either side lengths or area of a base and height? To what extent do they

- make sense of information given in a three-dimensional figure as it pertains to finding volume?
- model their understanding of finding volume conceptually and procedurally?
- describe how different types of information given about prisms can be used to determine volume?

Common Core Connection (CCSS.Math.Content.7.G.B.6)

Grade: Seventh

Domain: Geometry

Cluster:

Solve real-life and mathematical problems involving angle measure, area, surface area, and volume.

6. Solve real-world and mathematical problems involving area, volume, and surface area of two- and three-dimensional objects composed of triangles, quadrilaterals, polygons, cubes, and right prisms.

Uncovering Student Understanding About the Key Concepts

Using the Finding Volume Probe can provide the following information about how the students are thinking about area and volume measurements.

Do they		*Do they*
• have a conceptual and procedural understanding of area and volume?	OR	• use the volume formula as a procedural list of steps to follow to find an answer?
• correctly find volume, given a variety of types of information?	OR	• only process information if it is given in a way that fits nicely in the volume formula?

Exploring Excerpts From Educational Resources and Related Research

Common areas of difficulty for students:

Students often have preconceived ideas or even misconceptions and may know a list of steps or algorithms. Although they can perform these calculations, they may not always understand the concept or mathematical connections. (Hartweg, 2011, p. 41)

Students often confuse surface area and volume or have difficulty understanding the units they are measuring. (Hartweg, 2011, p. 43)

If [students] move rapidly to using formulas without an adequate conceptual foundation in area and volume, many students could have underlying confusions that would interfere with their working meaningfully with measurements. (NCTM, 2000, p. 242)

Surveying the Prompts and Selected Responses in the Probe

The Probe consists of four separate selected response items. The prompts and selected responses are designed to elicit understandings and common difficulties as described below:

If a student chooses	It is likely that the student
1b, 2b, 3c, 4a (correct answers)	• understands volume conceptually and reasons about the information given to accurately use formulas [See Sample Student Responses 1 and 2]. *Look for indication of the student's understanding in the written explanations of how the student got the answer.*
All other answers	• does not have a conceptual understanding of volume and is using the formulas incorrectly. In the case of 1a and 2a, the student is adding the given numbers; in the case of 3a, the student is multiplying the three numbers as if the figure were a rectangular prism instead of having a triangular base. Because the height of the base is not given in 3, neither the area of the base nor the volume can be found [See Sample Student Responses 3 and 4].

*T*eaching Implications and Considerations

Ideas for eliciting more information from students about their understanding and difficulties:

- What is area and/or surface area?
- What units are used to find area and surface area?
- What units are used to find volume?
- How are area and volume related? How are they different?
- What extra information is needed to find the volume of a figure (prism) if given the area of its base?
- Can you estimate the volume of the prisms?
- How is finding the volume of a rectangular prism similar/different from finding the volume of a triangular prism?

Ideas for planning instruction in response to what you learned from the results of administering the Probe:

- Emphasis should be on understanding the concepts of area and volume rather than on applying formulas.
- Geometric formulas should be learned through exploration and discovery.
- Students should be able to make connections between a formula and an actual object.
- Students can be at different levels of sophistication concerning [length, area, and volume]. The assumption that students can and must learn about length concepts first, then area concepts, then volume concepts frequently does not hold true. (NCTM, 1993, p. 79)

Sample Student Responses to Finding Volume

Responses That Suggest Understanding

Sample Student Response 1

Probe Item 1. b. Volume is length times width times height so $10 \times 6 \times 4$ is 240 m^3.

Probe Item 2. b. Because we are given the area of the front we only have to multiply that by the depth to get the volume so it would be $24 \times 4 = 96$ cm^3.

Probe Item 4. a. This is the same thing as number 2 . . . the base times the height. $40 \times 7 = 280$ m^3.

Sample Student Response 2

Probe Item 3. c. At first I was just going to multiply the 3 numbers together, but then I remembered I needed to find the area of the base and multiply that by the height. I don't know the height of the triangle so I can't find the area of the base. If I knew that I could figure it out.

Responses That Suggest Difficulty

Sample Student Response 3

Probe Item 2. c. There is not enough information. I need the height, width, and length of the cube.

Probe Item 4. c. I can't do this one either without having the measurements of the triangle.

Sample Student Response 4

Probe Item 3. a. This is the same as number 1. Multiple the three numbers together to get 480 m^2.

Variation: Volume of the Box

6.3V

Circle the correct answer.	Explain your choice.
1. 6 m 3 m 10 m a. 28 m³ b. 180 m³ c. I can't determine the volume	
2. 30 square meters 4 m a. 34 m³ b. 120 m³ c. I can't determine the volume	

Scale

Two students are working together on a missing measure problem.

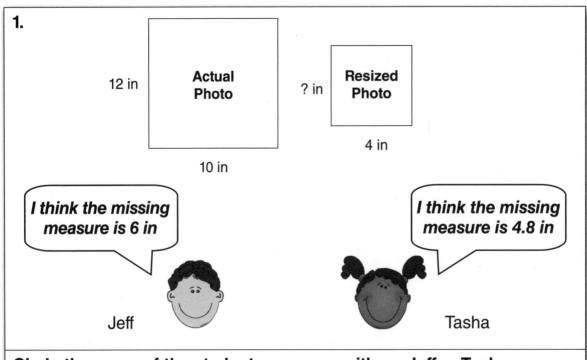

Circle the name of the student you agree with: Jeff   Tasha

Justify your choice:

Teacher Notes:
Scale

Questions to Consider About the Key Mathematical Concepts

When solving problems involving scale drawings, can students use concepts of similarity and proportional reasoning to find a missing side length? To what extent do they

- make sense of a scale drawing and proportional ratios?
- model how to use properties of similarity and proportional reasoning to find a missing side length of a figure scaled down from an original?
- describe the process used to find the side lengths of the transformation?

Common Core Connection (CCSS.Math.Content.7.G.A.1)

Grade: Seventh

Domain: Geometry

Cluster:

Draw, construct, and describe geometrical figures and describe the relationships between them.

1. Solve problems involving scale drawings of geometric figures, including computing actual lengths and areas from a scale drawing and reproducing a scale drawing at a different scale.

Uncovering Student Understanding About the Key Concepts

Using the Scale Probe can provide the following information about how the students are thinking about equivalent ratios and scale drawings.

Do they

- set up a proportion to find the missing side length?

- show understanding that the new figure is a similar figure scaled down by a specific amount (multiplicative relationship)?

OR

OR

Do they

- incorrectly reason about the length of the missing side?

- see the new figure as having an amount subtracted from each side (additive relationship)?

Do they

- use relationships within a ratio and between two ratios to solve for the missing side?

OR

Do they

- only see the relationship within a ratio?

Exploring Excerpts From Educational Resources and Related Research

Common areas of difficulty for students:

Students must recognize the difference between absolute, or additive, and relative, or multiplicative, change. (Langrall & Swafford, 2000, p. 258)

[Students] lack concrete and visual conceptions of proportion and size. [They] approach scaling problems by adding an equal amount to each dimension. (Stepans et al., 2005, pp. 52–53)

The ratio nature of measurement is trivial to people who have a quantitative scheme of measurement, but it is nontrivial to students who are building one. (NCTM, 2003, p. 101)

Being able to perform mechanical operations with proportions does not necessarily mean the students understand the underlying ideas of proportional thinking . . . the ability to firmly understand proportionality is a turning point in mental development. (NCTM, 1993, p. 160)

Surveying the Prompts and Selected Responses in the Probe

The Probe consists of one math talk item. The prompts and selected responses are designed to elicit understandings and common difficulties as described below:

If a student chooses	It is likely that the student
Tasha (correct answer)	• reasons the problem as a multiplicative relationship between the side lengths of the actual photo and the resized one (or between the two sides of the actual photo and the two of the resized) [See Sample Student Responses 1 and 2]. *Look for indication of the student's understanding in the written explanations of how the student got the answer.*

If a student chooses	It is likely that the student
Jeff	• misunderstands the relationship between the two photos or between each photo's sides as additive. The student reasons $12 - 10 = 2$, and $6 - 4 = 2$ or $10 - 4 = 6$ so $12 - 6 = 6$ [See Sample Student Responses 3 and 4].

Teaching Implications and Considerations

Ideas for eliciting more information from students about their understanding and difficulties:

- How can you compare the side lengths in the original photo?
- Which side of the original photo corresponds to the missing side of the new photo?
- Can you compare a side length of the original to a corresponding side in the smaller photo?
- Is the smaller photo similar to the larger one? In what ways?
- Is the similarity of the two photos multiplicative or additive?

Ideas for planning instruction in response to what you learned from the results of administering the Probe:

- Use manipulatives and technology as tools to help students learn similarity and ratio concepts in transformations.
- Begin instruction with situations that can be visualized or modeled.
- Students should understand that a proportional relationship occurs when there is a scale factor involved (multiplication not addition).
- Help students understand how to measure change in relationship with each other by introducing qualitative comparisons before numerical comparisons or missing values are found.
- Proportional reasoning should be developed over time, not in one unit.

Sample Student Responses to Scale

Responses That Suggest Understanding

Sample Student Response 1

I think Tasha is right. I set up a proportion and solved it. $\frac{12}{10} = \frac{x}{4} \rightarrow 10x = 48, x = 4.8$

Sample Student Response 2

Tasha is right because she must have done the right math to figure it out. $\frac{12}{x} = \frac{10}{4}$ Then to solve for x you cross multiply to get $10x = 48$, then divide by 10 to get $x = 4.8$.

Responses That Suggest Difficulty

Sample Student Response 3

I agree with Jeff because 12 − 10 = 2 so you have to do the same to the other sides. I figured out that 6 − 4 = 2 so 6 is the missing side.

Sample Student Response 4

Jeff is the right one. He did the right math. 10 − 4 is 6 so 12 − x = 6. When you solve for x you get 6.

Right Triangles

Three students are working together to determine whether the given triangles are right triangles.

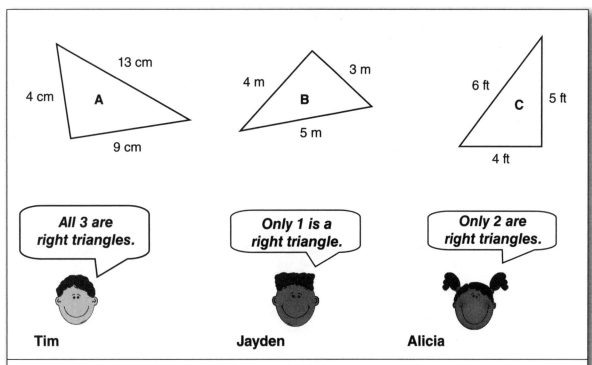

Circle the name of the student you agree with: Tim   Jayden   Alicia

Justify your choice:

Teacher Notes: Right Triangles

Questions to Consider About the Key Mathematical Concepts

When solving problems involving triangles, can students correctly use the Pythagorean Theorem converse to determine which ones are right triangles? To what extent do they

- make sense of and use the converse of the Pythagorean Theorem to determine whether triangles are right triangles?
- model the correct application of the Pythagorean Theorem?
- describe the reasoning and/or process they used for each figure shown?

Common Core Connection (CCSS.Math.Content.8.G.B.7)

Grade: Eighth

Domain: Geometry

Cluster:

Understand and apply the Pythagorean Theorem.

7. Apply the Pythagorean Theorem to determine unknown side lengths in right triangles in real-world and mathematical problems in two and three dimensions.

Uncovering Student Understanding About the Key Concepts

Using the Right Triangles Probe can provide the following information about how the students are thinking about right triangles.

Do they

- use properties of right triangles to prove (or disprove) whether figures are right triangles?

- use the Pythagorean Theorem correctly by squaring each side length first before comparing them?

OR

Do they

- use what the triangle looks like in the drawing to decide whether it is a right triangle?

- compare the side lengths without squaring them first?

Exploring Excerpts From Educational Resources and Related Research

Common areas of difficulty for students:

Secondary school students sometimes think of the longest side of a triangle as a hypotenuse. They assume the Pythagorean Theorem applies even when the triangle is not a right triangle. (Ashlock, 2006, p. 20)

From a *Boston Globe* article on the Massachusetts MCAS 10th grade math scores: The hardest question on the math section, which just 33 percent got right, asked students to calculate the distance between two points. It was a cinch—if students knew that they could plot the points and use the Pythagorean Theorem, a well-known formula to calculate the hypotenuse of a right triangle if the lengths of two legs are given. The sixth-hardest math question, which only 41 percent of students got right, also required use of the Pythagorean Theorem. "It seems applying the Pythagorean Theorem was a weakness for kids," said William Kendall, director of math for the Braintree public schools. "These weren't straightforward Pythagorean theorem questions. They had to do a little bit more" (Vaishnav, 2003). All three problems require students to transfer their understanding of the Pythagorean Theorem to a new situation. It is likely that most students in the United States could not do it, despite the fact that every set of state standards identifies a grasp of the Pythagorean Theorem as a key desired result (Wiggins, McTighe, & ASCD, 2005, p. 78).

Surveying the Prompts and Selected Responses in the Probe

The Probe consists of one math talk item. The prompts and selected responses are designed to elicit understandings and common difficulties as described below:

If a student chooses	*It is likely that the student*
Jayden (correct)	• understands the characteristics of a right triangle and the use of the Pythagorean Theorem converse to prove it. Triangle B is the only triangle that satisfies the Pythagorean Theorem and is therefore a right triangle [See Sample Student Response 1]. *Look for indication of the student's understanding in the written explanations of how the student got the answer.*

(Continued)

(Continued)

If a student chooses	It is likely that the student
Tim or Alicia	• does not fully understand the Pythagorean Theorem. For triangle A, the student does not square all the side lengths before adding the two smaller side lengths to see if it equals the square of the third, larger side length. Triangle C also does not satisfy the Pythagorean Theorem so is not a right triangle. In many cases students do not use the Pythagorean Theorem at all and use "intuitive rules," thinking that just because an angle looks to be 90° it must be a right angle, which in turn means a right triangle. Some students will not even consider Triangle B to be a right triangle because of its orientation [See Sample Student Responses 2, 3, 4, and 5].

Teaching Implications and Considerations

Ideas for eliciting more information from students about their understanding and difficulties:

- What theorem helps you determine whether triangles are right? What is the theorem? (leg^2 + leg^2 = hypotenuse^2) What do the "2s" tell us to do?
- If the triangles were right triangles, which sides would be the legs? The hypotenuse? How do you know that?

Ideas for planning instruction in response to what you learned from the results of administering the Probe:

- Often the Pythagorean Theorem is taught as a formula and a process used to solve for missing side lengths. Students should explore the properties of right triangles conceptually before applying the theorem.
- Instead of using $a^2 + b^2 = c^2$, which only works for triangles labeled ABC with angle C being the right angle, use leg^2 + leg^2 = hypotenuse^2, which holds more meaning for students and is generalized to work for all right triangles, regardless of their labeling.
- Students should be given opportunities to explore triangles in different ways (manipulatives, traditional manner, technology).

Sample Student Responses to Right Triangles

Responses That Suggest Understanding

Sample Student Response 1

Jayden is correct. The Pythagorean Theorem ($a^2 + b^2 = c^2$) only works with right triangles. $9^2 + 4^2 = 81 + 16 = 97$. $16^2 \neq 97$ so A is not a right triangle. $3^2 + 4^2 = 9 + 16 = 25$. $5^2 = 25$ so B is a right triangle. $4^2 + 5^2 = 16 + 25 = 41$. $6^2 \neq 41$ so C is not a right triangle. There is only one right triangle and that's triangle B.

Responses That Suggest Difficulty

Sample Student Response 2

I agree with Tim because all of the triangles should have a little square in the corner which means it's 90°. Also just by looking at them you can tell that they are 90°.

Sample Student Response 3

I agree with Tim because you can rotate each of the triangles to be a right triangle.

Sample Student Response 4

I agree with Jayden because triangle A is the only one that follows the Pythagorean Theorem ($a^2 + b^2 = c^2$). $4 + 9 = 13$.

Sample Student Response 5

Alicia is right because both A and C are right triangles, even though A is a little slanted it still has a right angle. B does not have a right angle.

Heights of Solids

Which of the following represents the height of the solid?

Height?	Explain your choice.
1. 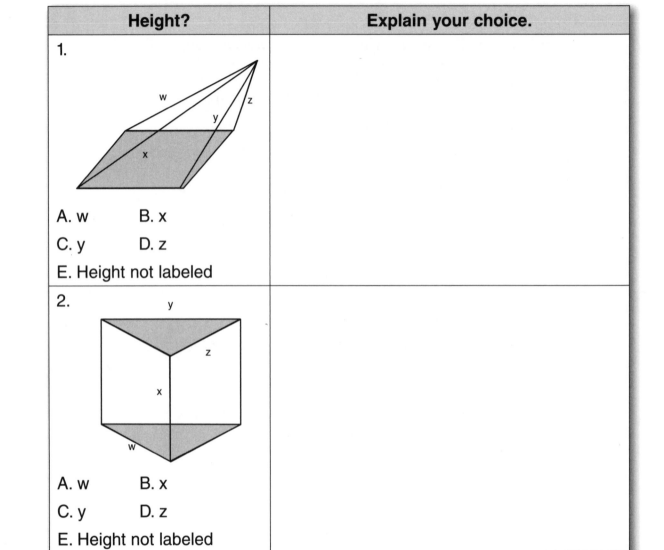 A. w B. x C. y D. z E. Height not labeled	
2. A. w B. x C. y D. z E. Height not labeled	
3. 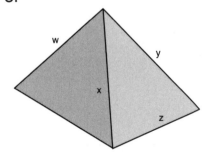 A. w B. x C. y D. z E. Height not labeled	

Teacher Notes: Heights of Solids

Questions to Consider About the Key Mathematical Concepts

When solving problems involving three-dimensional figures, can students determine how to find the height of the figure? To what extent do they

- make sense of the height of three-dimensional figures shown in a two-dimensional plane?
- model their visualization of three-dimensional figures?
- describe their reasoning on how to determine the height of three-dimensional figures?

Common Core Connection (CCSS.Math.Content.8.G.C.9)

Grade: Eighth

Domain: Geometry

Cluster:

Solve real-world and mathematical problems involving volume of cylinders, cones, and spheres.

9. Know the formulas for the volumes of cones, cylinders, and spheres and use them to solve real-world and mathematical problems.

Uncovering Student Understanding About the Key Concepts

Using the Heights of Solids Probe can provide the following information about how the students are thinking about three-dimensional figures.

Do they		*Do they*
• visualize the figures as representing three-dimensional objects?	OR	• see the figures as two dimensional?
• understand the difference between the height of an object and slant height?	OR	• interchange the two heights?

Do they

- correctly justify their reasoning when height is not labeled by including information on the actual height?

OR

Do they

- leave out information about the actual height when choosing "height not labeled"?

Exploring Excerpts From Educational Resources and Related Research

Common areas of difficulty for students:

Many students [are] focused on shallow knowledge and skills, not deep analysis using spatial reasoning and critical thinking. Students were more comfortable with flat surfaces that they could see on activity sheets or draw on their papers. It was not as easy for them to represent a three-dimensional surface on a two-dimensional plane. (Circello & Filkins, 2012, p. 341)

Even when an object's attribute is clear, the matter of conceiving its measure can still remain. (NCTM, 2003, p. 100)

[Students] have insufficient experiences in visualizing two- and three-dimensional models and lack understanding of concepts related to area and volume and the derivation of the formulas used to calculate them. (Stepans et al., 2005, p. 106)

Surveying the Prompts and Selected Responses in the Probe

The Probe consists of three separate selected response items. The prompts and selected responses are designed to elicit understandings and common difficulties as described below:

If a student chooses	It is likely that the student
1E, 2B, 3E (correct answer)	• can visualize three-dimensional figures to make conclusions about the height of an actual object [See Sample Student Response 1]. *Look for indication of the student's understanding in the written explanations of how the student got the answer.*

If a student chooses	It is likely that the student
All other answers	• is not accurately visualizing three-dimensional figures to analyze the actual figure. The student possibly is not using drawing cues to decide the height of an object [See Sample Student Responses 2, 3, and 4].

Teaching Implications and Considerations

Ideas for eliciting more information from students about their understanding and difficulties:

- What is the base of the three-dimensional figure? Is the figure "sitting" on its base?
- Can you imagine a figure in real life that might look similar to the figure shown?
- How would you determine the height of the real-life object?
- What is the difference between the height and the slant height of an object?

Ideas for planning instruction in response to what you learned from the results of administering the Probe:

- Students should develop visualization skills through hands-on experiences with a variety of geometric objects and through the use of technology that allows them to turn, shrink, and deform two- and three-dimensional objects. (NCTM, 2000, p. 43)
- Have students cut out nets of three-dimensional figures to create an actual model of the figure. This allows students to have a better understanding of what they are looking at when it is drawn two dimensionally.
- Allow students to use actual three-dimensional figures to solve problems.
- "The ability to construct two- and three-dimensional mental models from images is critical to developing understanding of formulas and skills in calculating these measurements" (Stepans et al., 2005, p. 108).
- Have group or class discussions on how to determine the heights of various objects and why most of the side lengths are not considered heights.
- Have students look at an object's shadow at different angles to see what the height looks like based on the orientation of the representation.
- Have students clarify what the base of a three-dimensional figure is.

Sample Student Responses to Heights of Solids

Responses That Suggest Understanding

Sample Student Response 1

Probe Item 1. E. Height is the length of something going straight up and down (perpendicular). None of these lines go straight up and down. . . . They are all slanted.

Probe Item 2. B. The height is B because that is how high the prism is. The other letters are part of the prism's base.

Probe Item 3. E. The height of a pyramid is from the center of the base to the vertex. You would have to "see" inside of the figure and have a dotted line from the top straight down to the bottom.

Responses That Suggest Difficulty

Sample Student Response 2

Probe Item 1. D. The height is D . . . it shows how high it is.

Sample Student Response 3

Probe Item 1. All of them are the height in their own way. E should say all of the above.

Probe Item 3. I think it is A, B, and C. All three of them show the height. D isn't the height though.

Sample Student Response 4

Probe Item 1. B. B is the height because it is the longest line.

Parallelograms

Three students are working together to determine whether a given shape is a parallelogram.

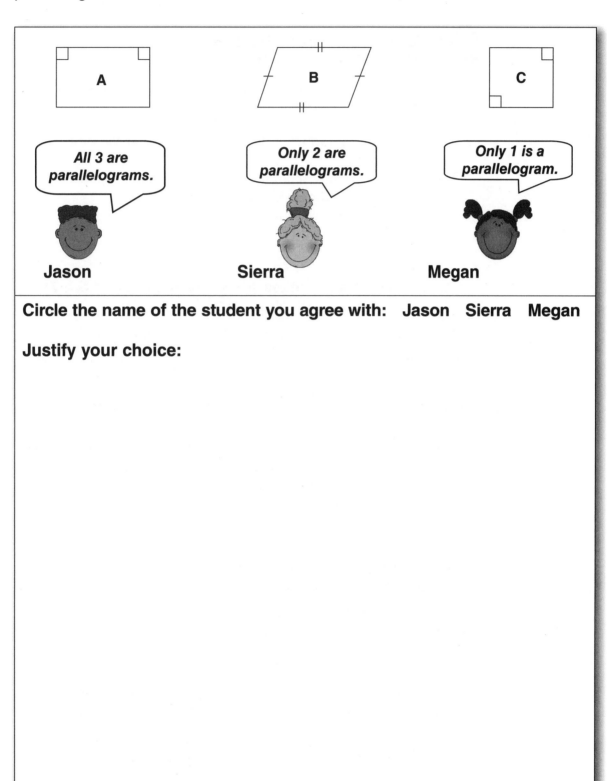

A

B

C

All 3 are parallelograms.

Jason

Only 2 are parallelograms.

Sierra

Only 1 is a parallelogram.

Megan

Circle the name of the student you agree with: Jason   Sierra   Megan

Justify your choice:

Teacher Notes: Parallelograms

Questions to Consider About the Key Mathematical Concepts

When solving problems involving geometric shapes, can students recognize parallelograms? To what extent do they

- make sense of information given in a figure and the properties of parallelograms?
- use what they know about the properties of parallelograms and the ways to prove if a figure is a parallelogram?
- describe what information is needed to determine whether a figure is a parallelogram?

Common Core Connection (CCSS.Math.Content.7.G.A.2)

Grade: Seventh

Domain: Geometry

Cluster:

Draw, construct, and describe geometrical figures and describe the relationships between them.

2. Draw (freehand, with ruler and protractor, and with technology) geometric shapes with given conditions. Focus on constructing triangles from three measures of angles or sides, noticing when the conditions determine a unique triangle, more than one triangle, or no triangle.

Uncovering Student Understanding About the Key Concepts

Using the Parallelograms Probe can provide the following information about how the students are thinking about properties of parallelograms.

Do they
- correctly use the information given on angle measures?   OR

- use properties of parallelograms to determine whether the figures are parallelograms?   OR

Do they
- make assumptions on what the unlabeled angle measures are?

- make decisions based on the appearance of the figures?

Exploring Excerpts From Educational Resources and Related Research

Common areas of difficulty for students:

Although eighth-grade students believe that parallel lines should not intersect and should be equidistant, they also believe that parallel segments must be aligned and that curves might be parallel (Mansfield & Happs, 1992). (NCTM, 2003, p.164)

There are many different ways of classifying geometric shapes, Students have difficulty identifying and describing the defining properties of a classification. (Stepans et al., 2005, p. 233)

Students can sometimes create improper generalizations based on life experiences. (Stepans et al., 2005, p. 234)

Surveying the Prompts and Selected Responses in the Probe

The Probe consists of one math talk item. The prompts and selected responses are designed to elicit understandings and common difficulties as described below:

If a student chooses	It is likely that the student
Megan (correct answer)	• understands the properties of parallelograms and can reason about the measures of the missing angles in the first and last triangles [See Sample Student Responses 1 and 2]. *Look for indication of the student's understanding in the written explanations of how the student got the answer.*
Jason or Sierra	• is assuming that the missing angle measures in figures A and C are 90°. Although they look like 90°, it cannot be assumed they are. Some students will not recognize that both pairs of opposite sides being congruent is proof for a parallelogram (as in figure B) [See Sample Student Responses 3, 4, and 5].

Teaching Implications and Considerations

Ideas for eliciting more information from students about their understanding and difficulties:

- What information can you tell me about the angles? How do you know that?
- What information do the marks on the figures tell you?
- What are the different ways to determine whether a figure is a parallelogram?

Ideas for planning instruction in response to what you learned from the results of administering the Probe:

- Students should generate properties and characteristic of parallelograms through inquiry with manipulatives or technology.
- Students should be taught that they cannot assume anything in geometry.
- When drawing figures for students, much care should be taken in accurately labeling information that is given and not allowing students to assume a right angle because it looks like one.
- Show students how the first and last quadrilaterals can take on a completely different look when the missing angles are drawn with measures that do not appear to be 90°.

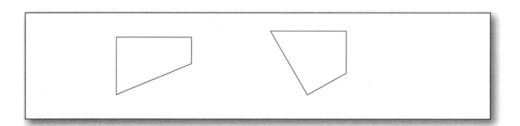

Sample Student Responses to Parallelograms

Responses That Suggest Understanding

Sample Student Response 1

Megan. I agree with Megan as I think the only one that is a parallelogram is B. If you have opposite sides congruent then it makes a parallelogram. The other two figures need to have the other angles labeled to know what their measures are.

Sample Student Response 2

Megan. Figure A could be but it might not be, too. One of the bottom angles could be 87 and the other one could be 93. Same with figure C . . . we don't know anything about the other two angles. I choose Megan because I know that B is a parallelogram.

Responses That Suggest Difficulty

Sample Student Response 3

Jason. A is a rectangle which is a special type of parallelogram, B is a plain parallelogram, and C is a square which is another special type of parallelogram.

Sample Student Response 4

Sierra. B and C are the only ones that are parallelograms. We don't know about A . . . the bottom line could be a little slanted.

Sample Student Response 5

Sierra. As A and C have all 90° angles they are parallelograms. I don't know anything about the angles in B so cannot assume it is a parallelogram.

Variation: Is It a Parallelogram?

Circle Yes or No.	Explain your choice.
a. Yes No	
b. Yes No	
c. Yes No	
d. Yes No	
e. Yes No	

7

Additional Considerations

An assessment activity can help learning if it provides information that teachers and their students can use as feedback in assessing themselves and one another and in modifying the teaching and learning activities in which they are engaged. (Black, Harrison, Lee, Marshall, & Wiliam, 2004, p. 10)

Mathematics Assessment Probes represent an approach to diagnostic assessment. They can be used for formative assessment purposes if the information about students' understandings and misunderstandings is used in a way that moves students' learning forward. There is a wide range of considerations in this chapter, including using the Probes to

- establish learning targets,
- allow for individual reflection,
- give student interviews,
- address individual needs,
- promote math talk,
- support the mathematical practices, and
- build capacity among teachers within and across grade levels.

Since the first Uncovering Student Thinking resource was in development, we have worked with and learned from the many teachers who have implemented our assessment Probes or have developed their own assessment Probes to use in their classrooms. Observing classes, trying out strategies ourselves with students, and listening to teachers describe their experiences and approaches have helped us capture various images from practice over time. The vignettes that accompany each of the considerations are chosen to highlight features of a particular instructional approach.

ESTABLISHING LEARNING TARGETS

> Stating and sharing intended outcomes of learning and assessment is really the foundation for all formative assessment activities. (Wylie et al., 2012, p. 22)

Establishing learning targets and sharing criteria for success in meeting the target is the foundation of the embedded formative assessment process (CCSSO, 2008; Heritage, 2010; Moss & Brookhart, 2012; Wiliam, 2011; Wylie et al., 2012). The need to develop students' content knowledge, including knowledge of the important mathematics concepts, procedures, and skills outlined in the Common Core State Standards for Mathematics, is a priority for mathematics educators. In order for students to meet these established expectations, instruction and assessment must take place with a clear, learning target in mind. Standards should inform teachers' thinking about learning targets as an interconnected cluster of learning goals that develop over time. By clarifying the specific ideas and skills described in the standards and articulating them as specific lesson-level learning targets aligned to criteria for success, teachers are in a better position to uncover the gap between students' existing knowledge or skill and the knowledge or skill described in the learning target and criteria for success.

Assessment Probe Use Related to Learning Targets

Each assessment Probe addresses a key mathematical idea aligned to Common Core State Standards for Mathematics, providing an example of how subsets of mathematics standards can be developed as learning goals. The example in Figure 7.1, from the Estimating Quotient Probe, highlights two components of the Teacher Notes helpful in determining learning targets: Questions to Consider About the Key Mathematic Concepts, and the connections to the Common Core State Standards for Mathematics.

Many teachers we work with are establishing learning targets on a daily basis and are using the Probes as tools to both support the development of a learning target prior to a lesson and to help students reach the learning target during a lesson.

When using a Probe to support the development of a learning target prior to a lesson, teachers give the Probe to students one to three days prior to the upcoming lesson or unit of instruction. They analyze the evidence gathered from the assessment to gauge students' current understandings and misunderstandings, and use this information to develop a learning target or set of learning targets.

Figure 7.1 Excerpts From Teacher Notes for Estimating Quotients

Questions to Consider About the Key Mathematical Concepts

When solving problems involving the division of decimals, can students reason about the size of the numbers and the effect of the operation to determine a reasonable estimate? To what extent do they

- reason correctly about the size of the divisor and dividend?
- determine whether the quotient will be smaller or larger than the dividend?
- describe how to use this reasoning to determine an estimate?

Common Core Connection (CCSS.Math. Content.6.NS.B.2 and CCSS.Math.Content.6.NS.B.3)

Grade: Sixth

Domain: The Number System

Clusters:

Compute fluently with multi-digit numbers and find common factors and multiples.

2. Fluently divide multi-digit numbers using the standard algorithm.

3. Fluently add, subtract, multiply, and divide multi-digit decimals using the standard algorithm for each operation.

Uncovering Student Understanding About the Key Concepts

Using the Estimating Quotients Probe can provide the following information about how the students are thinking about the effect of operating with decimals.

Do they

- correctly reason about the size of the dividend and divisor?

OR

Do they

- apply incorrect place value thinking?

- correctly reason about the size of the quotient?

OR

- apply an overgeneralization of "division always results in a smaller answer"?

- use reasoning about the size of the decimals and the effect of the division?

OR

- revert to applying an algorithm rather than using reasoning to determine an estimate?

The following image from practice provides an example of using a Probe prior to the start of a lesson or set of lessons.

In preparation for beginning work with the division of decimals by decimals, I wanted to get a sense of what my students already knew related to the idea. We had already spent some time discussing and exploring division of a decimal by a whole number so I was curious about whether students would apply this reasoning to choose an estimate when the divisor was also a decimal.

By reviewing the students' answers and explanations I found the following:

- When students included information in their explanations about the size of the numbers, students were able to judge the size of the decimal correctly with the exception of 0.04. Many described 0.04 as "smaller than 1" so I wasn't sure if they were thinking of the size of the number correctly.
- Even though students had seen a few problems in which the whole number divisor was larger than the dividend, more than half the students chose answers based on thinking that the estimate should be smaller than the dividend.
- Two students completed the division calculations using the standard algorithm; each made a mistake, although on different problems.

Based on these results, I decided on the following next steps:

- Begin with a review of the differences in sizes of 10th and 100th using 10 x 10 grids.
- Design the first learning target to focus on the effect of dividing with divisors that are smaller than the dividend. I will scaffold items from whole #'s divided by whole #'s, decimals by whole #'s, whole #'s by decimals, and decimals by decimals using numbers that can be modeled "nicely."
- Design the second learning target to focus on estimating decimal quotients with a range in sizes of the dividends and divisors.
- Design the third learning target to focus on using an algorithm to divide and to judge the reasonableness of the results. I will scaffold to more difficult numbers but even the difficult problems won't be "complex" (e.g., dividing by 0.03 rather than 0.235).

Incorporating the Probe prior to preparing for a section in a unit helps me think about a starting point, what I might emphasize, and who may need additional support on prerequisite ideas.

When using a Probe as a tool within a lesson or set of lessons, teachers first establish an alignment between the Probe content and the established learning target. In addition, they design instructional activities to support predicted understandings and misunderstandings likely to be uncovered by the Probe.

I noticed that my students were having difficulty with the steps involved in solving proportions and were unable to judge if their answer makes sense for the relationship involved. I decided to create a lesson around the use of the Estimates: Solving Proportions Probe to help support students' understanding of the meaning of a proportion and to provide the skills necessary for checking the reasonableness of their answers.

I started the lesson by introducing the learning target: "I will learn how reasoning about the relationship shown in a given ratio can help me estimate the value of a missing quantity in a proportion." I then asked the students to consider the target and gave them time to complete the Probe individually. While they were completing their second explanation, I asked the students to write their selected answers on a yellow sticky note, gathered the notes, and created a sticky bar chart of the results (see Figure 7.2).

Pointing to the sticky bar chart, I asked the students what they noticed and went on to discuss several new examples focusing on the content of the learning target. After this whole group discussion, students met in groups of four to follow up on the Probe items. Finally, I asked students to individually rewrite their choices and explanations on the back of the Probe and to write their choices on pink sticky notes. With the new sticky bar chart created next to the old, I asked random students to share their explanations and for the class to reflect on whether the explanation provided evidence of meeting the target.

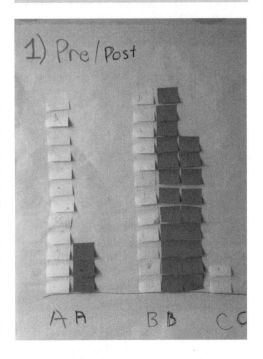

Figure 7.2 Sticky Bar Chart

INDIVIDUAL METACOGNITION AND REFLECTION (THE 4Cs)

> The Conceptual Change Model begins with having students become aware of their own thinking. Through a series of developmental steps, it helps them to confront their views and to refine them if necessary, then to immediately use their new understanding. (Stepans et al., 2005, p. 37)

The conceptual change model as described by Stepans and colleagues (2005) takes into consideration recommendations from research and is rooted in the learning cycle approach. The goal of the conceptual change model is to uncover students' current ideas about a topic before teaching new content related to the topic. Students learn by integrating new knowledge with what they already know and can do. Sometimes this new knowledge is integrated in a way that contributes to or builds on an existing misunderstanding. Through the Conceptual Change approach, since ideas are elicited prior to instruction, existing preconceptions and/or misconceptions can be confronted explicitly, minimizing situations in which students are trying to integrate new knowledge into a flawed or underdeveloped framework of ideas. This explicit confrontation of preconceptions or misconceptions creates cognitive dissonance in which students begin to question and rethink their preconceptions, and further instruction and reflection can now help students understand the new concept. Our 4Cs Model, an adaptation of the conceptual change model, consists of four stages, as is shown in Figure 7.3.

At this point, you may be wondering how the 4Cs Model connects with the QUEST Cycle. The QUEST Cycle is written from a teacher's point of view and implicitly incorporates the 4Cs Model. Since even the most effective teachers cannot do the actual learning for their students, the 4Cs Model provides the critical student perspective.

Figure 7.3 The 4Cs Model

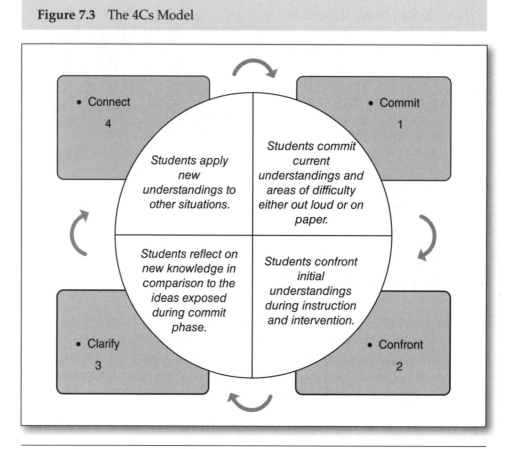

Source: Tobey and Fagan (2013).

Assessment Probe Use Related to the 4Cs Model

Teachers using the 4Cs Model in conjunction with assessment Probes typically use the following process:

1. *Commit.* Choose a Probe to elicit ideas related to a learning target. Give the Probe to all students, capturing student responses either by asking them to write explanations, scripting their explanations, or a combination of both.

2. *Confront.* Provide instruction based on results, integrating a variety of anonymous student responses, both correct and incorrect, into the lesson at appropriate junctures and lead class discussion about the responses.

3. *Clarify.* Return students' initial responses to the Probe to them (or read them to students) and ask students to clarify or revise anything in the response based on what they just learned in the lesson.

4. *Connect.* Pose additional questions similar to those in the Probe to assess whether students have met the learning target.

The image on page 179 about using the Estimate: Solving Proportions to help students meet the learning target provides one image of engaging students in the 4Cs Model. The following image from practice highlights an additional use.

This year I have created a routine of giving students a Probe, collecting the Probe, and returning the Probe when I felt students were ready to reflect and revise. Establishing this as a routine has helped students understand the meaning of diagnostic assessment and has provided buy-in for the use of the Probes. I think this buy-in is based on being explicit with students that the Probes are for me to consider where to go with instruction and for them to be able to see their own growth in understanding related to a topic. When the students get their original Probe back, whether it is during the same lesson, a day later, or several days later, they will know what is expected of them. Along with the Probe, I pass out colored pencils or pens. They use the different color to circle their response (or recircle their previous response) and then revamp their former explanations based on their new understandings. On the back of the Probe they reflect on their growth by describing the difference between the original response/explanation and the new response/explanation.

GIVING STUDENT INTERVIEWS

Whenever we try to get at a student's thinking, we should try to focus not only on what the student is thinking but also on what the student understands about his or her own knowledge. The questions we ask when interviewing a student will help the student become more aware of her own cognitive processes. (Ashlock, 2006, p. 27)

Conducting individual or small group interviews provides information beyond what written student work can provide. Interviewing students offers insight into their level of understanding and their ability to put mathematical ideas into words and/or representations. The interview process also allows teachers to gather information about the range of learning needs within a group of students. Teachers who regularly incorporate student interviews either selectively interview a subset of students or all of their students depending upon how they wish to use the results.

Assessment Probe Use Related to Student Interviews

Good interviewing requires careful preparation in advance, keeping in mind purposes, method of selection, environment, questions and follow-up probes, and uses. (Stepans et al., 2005, p. 277)

Teachers have found that any Probe can be administered as an interview; they see benefits to this mode of administration at any age.

Many teachers manage individual interviews by conducting them while their students not being interviewed are engaged in other activities. Teachers can also capitalize on a small group approach to "interview" multiple students individually as they simultaneously worked on the tasks of the Probe. When managed well, these conversations provide valuable information about students' thinking and their ability to build on the ideas of other students to advance their thinking. One challenge of the small group interview approach is the temptation to jump from information gathering to instruction. Stay focused on and be explicit with students that the goal of this small group activity is for you to listen to their ideas and ask questions in order to plan for a new learning experience on another day. Being explicit in this way avoids confusion for students who may also participate in small intervention groups or other small group work focused on instruction.

ADDRESSING INDIVIDUAL NEEDS

Although many teachers feel they lack the time or tools to pre-assess on a regular basis, the data derived from pre-assessment are essential in driving differentiated instruction. (Small, 2009, p. 5)

In addition to using Probes as preassessment, understanding how the math content contained in the Probe connects to a progression of math learning can support efforts to differentiate instruction to meet students' needs.

The Common Core State Standards in mathematics were built on progressions: narrative documents describing the progression of a topic across a number of grade levels, informed both by research on children's cognitive development and by the logical structure of mathematics. These documents were spliced together and then sliced into grade level standards. From that point on the work focused on refining and revising the grade level standards. The early drafts of the progressions documents no longer correspond to the current state of the standards. It is important to produce up-to-date versions of the progressions documents. They can explain why standards are sequenced the way they are, point out cognitive difficulties and pedagogical solutions, and give more detail on particularly knotty areas of the mathematics.

—http://ime.math.arizona.edu/progressions

Being aware of and understanding a progression of learning of a topic is important when considering how to address the needs of students. Often individual students can be grouped with others who have a similar misunderstanding or who have a similar missing foundational concept that is posing a barrier to learning the mathematics of the learning target. "Compiling an inventory for a set of papers can provide a sense of the class' progress and thus inform decisions about how to differentiate instruction" (Burns, 2005, p. 29). Decisions about next steps should be informed based on the goal of moving students' understanding toward a defined learning target; when the gap between existing knowledge and the learning target is too great, however, students may need to access the content at a "lower" point in the learning progression. This may require developing alternate and additional learning targets allowing students to build the prerequisite understanding necessary. Probes provide critical information to inform these decisions and are therefore a useful tool for all teachers of math, including special educators, Title I teachers, and interventionists.

PROMOTING MATH TALK

Because discussions help students to summarize and synthesize the mathematics they are learning, the use of student thinking is a critical element of mathematical discourse. When teachers help students build on their thinking through talk, misconceptions are made clearer to both teacher and student, and at the same time, conceptual and procedural knowledge deepens. (Garcia, 2012, p. 3)

Talking the talk is an important part of learning. (Black & Harrison, 2004, p. 4)

When students are talking about their mathematical ideas—whether in a whole-class discussion, in small groups, or in pairs—they are using the language and conventions of mathematics.

Children learn vocabulary primarily indirectly through their conversations with others and from the books and programs they are exposed to. However, because many words used in mathematics may not come up in everyday contexts—and if they do, they may mean something totally different—math vocabulary needs to be explicitly taught. Students' use of math terms is directly related to their experiences. Lack of exposure to math situations and opportunities to develop a correct mathematical vocabulary can deprive students of the language of math. The language of math is specific and uses words to denote not only meaning but also symbolic notation. Symbols enable mathematical ideas to be expressed in precise ways that reflect quantitative relationships. Misunderstandings about the meaning of a math symbol or notation or how to use it can impact understanding. Just as some words can take on different meanings in different contexts, so can some mathematical symbols.

Assessment Probe Use Related to Promoting Math Talk

In Chapter 1, we used an image from practice to illustrate how assessment Probes can create a link between assessment, instruction, and learning. We remind you of that image here:

> In a Grade 8 classroom, students are engaged in a class discussion to decide whether a given relationship shown in a table, graph, or equation is proportional. After using a card sort strategy to individually group cards as "Proportional" and "Not Proportional," the teacher encourages the students to develop a list of characteristics that could be used to decide whether a relationship is proportional. As students share their ideas and come to an agreement, the teacher records the characteristic and draws an example and nonexample to further illustrate the idea for each type of representation. He then gives students an opportunity to regroup their cards, using the defining characteristics they have developed as a class. As the students discuss the results of their sorting process, the teacher listens for and encourages students to use the listed characteristics to justify their choices. Throughout the discussion, the class works together to revise the characteristics already listed and to add additional characteristics that were not included in the initial discussion. (Adapted from Keeley & Rose Tobey, 2011)

The image illustrates how a teacher engages students in discussion using the examples and nonexamples to tease out characteristics of proportional relationships within tables, graphs, equations, and problem contexts. The book from which this excerpt is taken, *Mathematics Formative Assessment: 75 Practical Strategies for Linking Assessment, Instruction and Learning,* provides descriptions of specific strategies that can be combined with assessment Probes in order to promote learning through mathematical discourse (Keeley & Rose Tobey, 2011). Many of these strategies have been used or modified for use in conjunction with Probes. Two such strategies, Agreement Circles and the more commonly used Think-Pair-Share, provide a whole group strategy example and a pair/small group example of promoting learning through discourse.

Agreement Circles

Agreement Circles provide a kinesthetic way to activate thinking and engage students in discussing and defending their mathematical ideas. Students stand in a large circle as the teacher reads a statement. The students who agree with the statement step to the center of the circle. Those who disagree remain standing on the outside of the circle. Those in the inner circle face their peers still standing around the outside circle and then divide themselves into small groups of students who agree and disagree. The small groups then engage in discussion to defend their thinking. This is repeated with several rounds of statements relating to the same topic, each time with students starting by standing around the large circle. At the beginning, this strategy works best with Probes that generated substantial disagreement. Over time, once the classroom environment allows for students to take risks and feel safe doing so, the strategy can be successfully used when a smaller range of students choose certain selected responses. (Keeley & Rose Tobey, 2011, pp. 54–55)

Think-Pair-Share

Think-Pair-Share begins by providing students with an opportunity to activate their own thinking. The pairing strategy allows students to first share their ideas with one other person and modify their ideas or construct new knowledge as they interact with their partner. Next, students are asked to share ideas with a larger group. After having had a chance to discuss their ideas with another student as a pair, many students are more comfortable and willing to respond to the whole-group discussion. As a result, the quality of their responses often improves and contributes to an improvement in the quality of the whole group discussion as well. Thoughtful pairing of student helps to ensure that the pair conversation is productive. Consider pairing students with others with whom they will engage productively and whose content level understanding is similar enough for common ground yet reflects differences that will evoke conversation.

In the Think-Square-Share variation, students discuss in groups of four rather than in pairs. When using a Probe with selected response choices, teachers can prearrange groups so that each includes students who chose different selections. In their "square," they have a chance to discuss their thinking and try to justify their reasoning or modify it based on information they gain from the discussion. (Keeley & Rose Tobey, 2011, pp. 189–190)

SUPPORTING THE MATHEMATICAL PRACTICES

Formative assessment begins by identifying a learning goal, based on a grade-level standard from the Common Core State Standards (CCSS). Since the grade-level standards in the CCSSM "define what students should understand and be able to do," it is important for teachers to find out what students know and can do both conceptually and procedurally in relation to the expectation for learning. In addition to these content standards, an important feature of the CCSSM is the Standards for Mathematical Practices. These practices describe a variety of processes and proficiencies that teachers at all grade levels should seek to develop in their students. Since the CCSSM does not define the methods and strategies used to determine the readiness and prior knowledge necessary to achieve the standards, the Mathematics Assessment Probes in this book complement CCSSM's eight Standards for Mathematical Practices and their link to mathematical content.

How the use of Probes supports each of the practice clusters (see Appendix B for more information about these clusters) is described below, beginning with the practices related to reasoning and explanation.

Assessment Probe Use Related to the "Reasoning and Explaining" Practice Cluster

Simply using the Mathematics Assessment Probes with students will not result in students who are proficient within this cluster of practices. Instead, use of the Probes over time, combined with higher expectations for reasons and justification for selecting a response, will support students as they progress toward proficiency. Use of the follow-up questions accompanying the Probes (see Figure 7.4 for an example) can help students who are having difficulty describing their reasoning or who give only brief explanations such as "I just knew" or "I learned that in class."

Since students naturally generalize from examples and nonexamples, many of the assessment Probes are structured or can be structured as card sorts, which capitalize on examples and nonexamples to help students build important reasoning skills. Middle school students are very able to use a variety of ways to justify their answers, including generating and organizing data to make, validate, or refute a conjecture and developing facility with inductive and deductive reasoning. The extent to which students are able to use these skills when giving explanations can be elicited through use of the Probes.

Figure 7.4 Estimate: Solving Proportions Follow-Up Questions

Teaching Implications and Considerations

Ideas for eliciting more information from students about their understanding and difficulties:

- What strategy are you going to use with estimating the decimals?
- How will estimating the decimals help with understanding the ratio? The proportion?
- What numbers are you going to compare to find x? Why?
- Are there more than one set of numbers you can compare to find the scale?

Some of the assessment Probes make use of the "math-talk" structure in which students are asked to decide who they agree with and provide a reason for their choice. Probes that are structured in this way provide opportunities for students to critique the reasonableness of another's answer and to justify their conclusions. Again, using Probes structured in this way only on occasion during the school year will not build students' ability in a meaningful way. Instead, students will need multiple opportunities over the course of the school year and across all of the mathematics domains in order to build these abilities.

While observing students work in pairs on comparing their cards under Proportional and Not Proportional, I captured various comments from students that demonstrated justification based on reasoning about the properties of proportional relationships as well as comments that did not. After the comparisons were complete, I displayed the following list of captured comments:

This line has a constant rate and is going through the origin.	It just looks right.
This story describes a constant rate but one not common starting point.	That is just like the problem we saw yesterday except yesterday was about running.
I looked for something that meant "per" because that means a rate. Then we have to look for the other part.	This word problem must be not proportional because it has a lot more words / is longer.
We need to extend the table to see if we get (0,0) and then we have to see if what is changing is always changing by the same amount.	This first column is by 5's and the second column by 20's.

(Continued)

(Continued)

I asked students to think about the difference between the comments in the left column and the comments in the right column. After a class discussion on the differences as well as what two pieces were common among all those in the left column, I handed out the recording sheet. I had adapted the recording sheet (see Figure 7.5) to request students choose a card from each pile that they were most sure and least sure of. Students worked independently on the recording sheet.

Figure 7.5 Recording Sheet

Proportional Cards	Explanation
Not Proportional Cards	**Explanation**

I often ask students if they agree with a classmate's strategy and/or solution and then follow up by asking several students why they agree or do not agree. This is a regular feature of our daily class discussions during math time and becomes a routine for students.

The Math Talk Probe structure mirrors this routine in a way that allows all students to respond simultaneously. When given a Math Talk Probe, students first complete the problem and then compare their responses to those of several fictitious students. If they agree with one of the fictitious student's responses, they then need to be able to explain *why* they agree.

> My periodical use of a Math Talk Probe "slows down the process," allowing more time for all students to reflect and communicate before any of them begin to share their thinking. In addition to providing this benefit for students, this Probe structure of "do, compare, choose, and explain" gives me a chance to scan students' choices more quickly to determine who may be struggling for a particular reason and what patterns are emerging across all of the student responses.
>
> I also use this Probe structure to design my own "math-talk" tasks as mini-assessments during or toward the end of a set of lessons. I use actual student responses that I have heard from the students during class discussions to create my own "math talk" responses.

When students derive answers to problems, we not only need to get at their thinking in order to understand how they obtained those answers, we also need to learn how they justify their answers—how they prove they are correct in their own thinking. We can look for three kinds of justification schemes identified by Sowder and Harel and illustrated by Flores:

- *Externally based schemes* in which a textbook or authority figure is cited as justification
- *Empirically based schemes* in which students use perception or concrete objects to show that their answer is correct
- *Analysis use schemes* in which students use strategies or state mathematical relations to justify their answer

As a student's thinking develops over time, we expect to see fewer uses of justification schemes that are externally based. We even hope to see use of empirically-based schemes eventually give way to schemes that use analysis, for such thinking is distinctly mathematical. (Ashlock, 2006, p. 28)

In summary, middle school students should be encouraged to make conjectures, be given time to search for evidence to prove or disprove them using inductive and deductive reasoning, and be expected to explain and justify their ideas. Students should be introduced to and be expected to use basic logic words in their explanation, including *if . . .*, *then . . .*, *and*, *or*, *not*, *all*, and *some*, and to incorporate mathematical properties and relationships, rather than authority (e.g., because my teacher told me), as the basis for the argument.

Assessment Probe Use Related to the "Seeing Structure and Generalizing" Practice Cluster

Many of the mathematics targets of the assessment Probes align to the CCSSM content standards directly associated with the Seeing Structure and Generalizing Practice Structure. For example, the Linear Equations Probe (see Figure 7.6) elicits from students whether they have generalized the relationships between representations of linear graphs and equations.

Figure 7.6   Linear Equations Probe

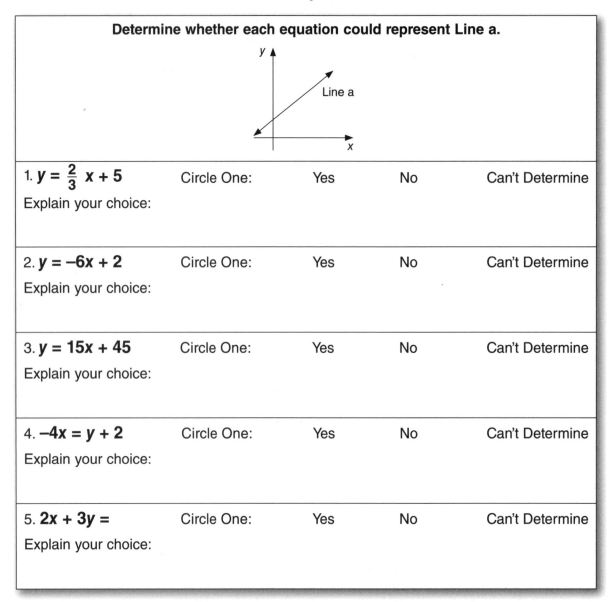

Linear Equations

Determine whether each equation could represent Line a.

1. $y = \frac{2}{3}x + 5$ Circle One: Yes   No   Can't Determine

Explain your choice:

2. $y = -6x + 2$ Circle One: Yes   No   Can't Determine

Explain your choice:

3. $y = 15x + 45$ Circle One: Yes   No   Can't Determine

Explain your choice:

4. $-4x = y + 2$ Circle One: Yes   No   Can't Determine

Explain your choice:

5. $2x + 3y =$ Circle One: Yes   No   Can't Determine

Explain your choice:

Students who are able to choose the correct responses are likely to be generalizing about the graph and equations. The Level 2 explanation is key to determining whether, in fact, students are using these generalizations and are able to explain or articulate the reasons for their correct responses.

In the Statistics Learning Progression document the authors state that by Grade 8, "Students now have enough experience with coordinate geometry and linear functions to plot bivariate data as points on a plane and to make use of the equation of a line in analyzing the relationship between two paired variables. They build statistical models to explore the relationship between two variables; looking for and making use of structure to describe possible association in bivariate data" (Common Core Standards Writing Team, 2011, p. 11). See Figure 7.7.

Figure 7.7 Scatterplots Probe

Scatterplots

Determine whether the data in each scatterplot shows a positive, negative, or no correlation or whether there isn't enough information to determine the correlation.

Circle the correct answer.	Explain your choice.
1. a. Positive b. Negative c. No correlation d. Not enough information	
2. a. Positive b. Negative c. No correlation d. Not enough information	
3. a. Positive b. Negative c. No correlation d. Not enough information	

Assessment Probe Use Related to the Modeling and Using Tools Practice Cluster

Many of the mathematical targets of the assessment Probes align to the Common Core content standards directly associated with the Modeling and Using Tools Practice Cluster. For example, the Writing Equations

Probe requires students to model a given situation with an equation (see Figure 7.8).

Choosing the correct equations for each item indicates that students are able to choose a mathematical model by translating the mathematical

Figure 7.8   Writing Equations Probe

Writing Equations

Choose the equation that best represents the statement. In each equation s represents the number of students and t represents the number of teachers.

Circle the correct answer.	Explain your choice.
1. **There are 45 more students than teachers on the field trip.** a. $45 = s + t$ b. $s + 45 = t$ c. $t + 45 = s$	
2. **There are 7 times as many students as teachers in the cafeteria today.** a. $7s = t$ b. $7t = s$ c. $st = 7$	
3. **There are 17 fewer teachers than students in the gym.** a. $17 - t = s$ b. $t - s = 17$ c. $s - t = 17$	

relationship into an equation, making sense of the words. Once again, it is the elaboration prompt that requires the students to describe their process and allows the teacher to get a better sense of the students' approach to modeling mathematically.

In addition to Probes that are directly connected to content standards related to modeling and/or the use of tools, all the assessment Probes have the ability to elicit information regarding this practice cluster. For many of the assessment Probes, there is not an expectation that a particular model or tool be used. At the diagnostic stage, more information is gathered about your students if you naturally allow students to request tools to use in determining their response and/or in explaining their thinking. An important consideration when using assessment Probes is to combine the use of Probes that expect specific modeling processes or given tools with Probes that expect more varied and open-ended approaches. In this way, you can provide opportunities for students to practice identifying and utilizing helpful tools and you can learn how their abilities in this area are progressing.

Assessment Probe Use Related to the Overarching Habits of Mind of Productive Thinkers Practice Cluster

The assessment Probes can support student metacognition by inviting students to identify the extent of their own understanding of a problem and its solution and to examine and make sense of the problem-solving approaches of others. The Probes relate to this overarching cluster of practices both in terms of the content of the Probes and the ways in which they are used in questioning, instruction, and discussion.

Mathematical Practices Summary

The ideas within the Mathematical Practices must be developed over time and throughout a student's K–12 school experience. "Doing mathematics means generating strategies for solving problems, applying those approaches, seeing if they lead to solutions, and checking to see whether your answers make sense" (Van de Walle, Karp, & Bay-Williams, 2013, p. 13). When students view mathematics as interpreting, organizing, inquiring about, and constructing meaning, it becomes creative and alive (Fosnot & Dolk, 2001, p. 13).

SHARING EXPERIENCES AND PROMOTING PROFESSIONAL COLLABORATION

The engine of improvement, growth, and renewal in a professional learning community is collective inquiry. The people in such a school are relentless in questioning the status quo, seeking new methods, testing those methods, and then reflecting on the results. (DuFour, DuFour, Eaker, & Many, 2006, p. 68)

Using Probes provides an opportunity for collaboration among educators as they examine and discuss student work together:

> The most important aspect of this strategy is that teachers have access to, and then develop for themselves the ability to understand, the content students are struggling with and ways that they, the teachers, can help. Pedagogical content knowledge—that special province of excellent teachers—is absolutely necessary for teachers to maximize their learning as they examine and discuss what students demonstrate they know and do not know. (Loucks-Horsley, Love, Stiles, Mundry, & Hewson, 2003, p. 183)

Looking at student work on Probes is a refreshing change from looking at student work and scoring with a rubric. We started looking at student work on Probes after our math curriculum coordinator introduced the idea as an option for our professional learning community work in which our focus was on action research in the classroom. The QUEST Cycle really fit the needs we had in using a common structure for our research.

We decided to alternate months: one month we choose a common Probe and the next month we each choose one on our own. During the common Probe month, we each bring student work to our PLC meeting and review a sampling from the whole set. We establish types of understanding and misunderstandings to look for and then work in pairs to review the work, keeping a running tally of each category. Each pair also looks for one to two interesting papers to share with the whole group. We come back together after reviewing the work to share our findings, review the interesting papers, and summarize next steps related to instruction.

On our individual Probe months, we each review our own student work, choose two to three papers of interest and summarize findings and next steps prior to the meeting. At the meeting, we meet in groups of three to share our experiences and to review each other's sample student papers.

By providing research sound bites and instructional implications specific to the ideas of the Probe, the Teacher Notes can guide educators through the action research QUEST Cycle, providing a collaborative framework for examining student thinking together and developing plans for improving instruction.

SUMMARY

An important takeaway about using the Probes is the importance of your role in selecting and scaffolding Probes for use in the classroom. When selecting Probes consider

- how well the content of the Probe aligns to the targeted concepts you want students to learn;

- how well the structure of the Probe lends itself to the mathematical practice you wish students to incorporate; and
- how the Probe will serve as the link between assessment, instruction, and learning.

The first of the considerations, targeting the appropriate math content, was discussed in Chapter 1, where we outlined conceptual and procedural understanding and highlighted where in the Teacher Notes to find information about concepts targeted through a Probe. The second consideration, targeting the ideas within the practices, was the focus of this chapter. The final consideration, providing the link to learning, is a thread that runs throughout the book.

If you are new to using assessment Probes, we suggest that you try a couple of Probes before returning to review the information in this chapter again after you have some firsthand experience. We also encourage you to visit **uncoveringstudentideas.org** to share experiences with others who are using Probes in mathematics and science. We look forward to hearing your ideas.

Appendix A

Information on the Standards for Mathematical Practice

The Standards for Mathematical Practice are not a checklist of teacher to-dos but rather support an environment in which the CCSS for mathematics content standards are enacted and are framed by specific expertise that you can use to help students develop their understanding and application of mathematics. (Larson, Lott Adams, Fennell, Dixon, & Kanold, 2012, p. 26)

Formative assessment begins by identifying a learning goal, such as a grade level expectation from the CCSSM. The Common Core State Standards for Mathematics define what students should understand and be able to do in K–12 mathematics. Since the grade-level expectations in the CCSS define what students should "understand" or "be able to do," it is important for teachers to find out what students know and can do both conceptually or procedurally in relation to the expectation for learning. In addition to these content standards, an important feature of the CCSSM is the Standards for Mathematical Practices. These practices describe a variety of processes, proficiencies, and dispositions that teachers at all grade levels should seek to develop in their students. Since the CCSS do not define the methods and strategies used to determine the readiness and prior knowledge necessary to achieve the standards, the Mathematics Assessment Probes in this book complement CCSS's eight Standards for Mathematical Practices and their link to mathematical content (adapted from Keeley & Rose Tobey, 2011, p. 30).

Figure A.1 The Progression Project's Structure of the Mathematics Standards

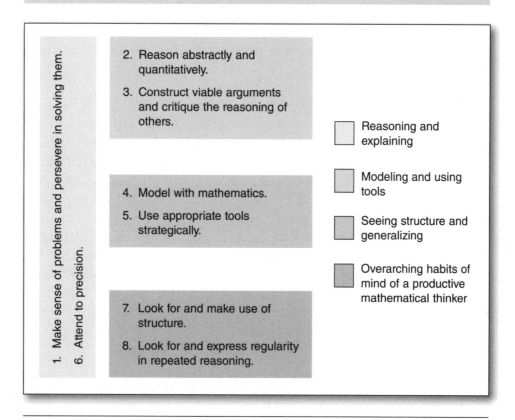

Source: McCallum (2011).

STRUCTURING THE MATHEMATICAL PRACTICE STANDARDS

The Institute for Mathematics and Education's Progression Project is organizing the writing of final versions of the progressions documents for the K–12 CCSS. The work is being done by members of the original team along with mathematicians and educators not involved in the initial writing of the standards (Institute for Mathematics and Education [IME], 2012). The Progression Project created the diagram in Figure A.1 to provide some higher order structure to the practice standards, in the way that the clusters and domains provide higher order structure to the content standards.

The remaining part of this appendix will address each of the practice clusters using language from a variety of resources including the Common Core document, the Common Core Learning Progressions documents, and the Unpacking documents created by North Carolina's Department of Public Instruction. In Chapter 7, we describe how the Probes can be used in relationship to the ideas of each cluster.

Reasoning and Explaining Practice Cluster (Practices 2 and 3)

Each of the Probes includes a selected answer response and an explanation prompt. These explanation prompts are the key to the practices within this cluster.

Mathematical Practice 2. Reason abstractly and quantitatively. Students demonstrate proficiency with this practice when they make sense of quantities and relationships while solving tasks. This involves both decontextualizing and contextualizing. When decontextualizing, students need to translate a situation into a numeric or algebraic sentence that models the situation. They represent a wide variety of real world contexts through the use of real numbers and variables in mathematical expressions, equations, and inequalities. When contextualizing, students need to pull from a task information to determine the mathematics required to solve the problem. For example, after a line is fit through data, students interpret the data by interpreting the slope as a rate of change in the context of the problem (CCSSO, 2010; Common Core Standards Writing Team, 2011–2012; North Carolina Department of Public Instruction, 2012a, 2012b, 2012c).

Students who reason abstractly and quantitatively are able to

- move from context to abstraction and back to context;
- make sense of quantities and their relationships in problem situations;
- use quantitative reasoning that includes creating a coherent representation of the problem at hand;
- consider the units involved;
- attend to the meaning of quantities (not just how to compute with them);
- know and flexibly use different properties of operations and objects; and
- use abstract reasoning when measuring and comparing the lengths of objects.

Mathematical Practice 3. Construct viable arguments and critique the reasoning of others. Students demonstrate proficiency with this practice when they accurately use mathematical terms to construct arguments, engage in discussions about problem-solving strategies, examine a variety of problem-solving strategies, and begin to recognize the reasonableness of them, as well as similarities and differences among them. Middle school students should construct arguments using oral or written explanations accompanied by expressions, equations, inequalities, models; and graphs, tables, and other data displays including box plots, dot plots, and histograms (CCSSO, 2010; Common Core Standards Writing Team, 2011–2012; North Carolina Department of Public Instruction, 2012a, 2012b, 2012c).

Students who construct viable arguments and critique the reasoning of others are able to

- make conjectures and build a logical progression of statements to explore the truth of their conjectures;
- recognize and use counterexamples;

- justify their conclusions, communicate them to others, and respond to the arguments of others;
- distinguish correct logic or reasoning from that which is flawed and, if there is a flaw in an argument, explain what it is;
- construct arguments using concrete referents such as objects, drawings, diagrams, and actions; and
- listen or read the arguments of others, decide whether they make sense, and ask useful questions to clarify or improve arguments, including "How did you get that?" "Is that always true?" and "Why does that work?"

Seeing Structure and Generalizing Practice Cluster (Practices 7 and 8)

Adolescents make sense of their world by looking for patterns and structure and routines. They learn by integrating new information into cognitive structures they have already developed.

Mathematical Practice 7. Look for and make use of structure. Students demonstrate proficiency with this practice when they look for patterns and structures in the number system and other areas of mathematics such as modeling problems involving properties of operations. Students examine patterns in tables and graphs to generate equations and describe relationships. For instance, students recognize proportional relationships that exist in ratio tables, double numbers, graphs, and equations describing the multiplicative properties. Students apply properties to generate equivalent expressions (e.g., distributive property and properties of exponents) and solve equations. In geometry, students compose and decompose two- and three-dimensional figures to solve real-world problems involving area and volume and explore the effects of transformations and describe them in terms of congruence and similarity (CCSSO, 2010; Common Core Standards Writing Team, 2011–2012; North Carolina Department of Public Instruction, 2012a, 2012b, 2012c).

Students who look for and make use of structure are able to

- identify patterns in various displays of distributions of univariate and bivariate data;
- describe the multiplicative properties of proportional relationships;
- measure the attributes of three-dimensional shapes, allowing them to apply area formulas to solve surface area and volume problems; and
- categorize shapes according to properties and characteristics.

Mathematical Practice 8. Look for and express regularity in repeated reasoning. Students demonstrate proficiency with this practice when they look for regularity in problem structures when problem solving, notice if calculations are repeated, and look for both general methods and shortcuts; use repeated reasoning to understand algorithms; and make generalizations about patterns. For example, they make connections between covariance, rates, and representations showing the relationships between quantities. They connect place value and prior work with operations to understand algorithms to fluently divide multi-digit numbers and perform all operations with multi-digit decimals. They use iterative processes to determine more-precise rational approximations for irrational numbers (CCSSO, 2010; Common Core Standards Writing Team, 2011–2012; North Carolina Department of Public Instruction, 2012a, 2012b, 2012c).

Students who "look for and express regularity in repeated reasoning" are able to

- notice if processes are repeated;
- look for both general methods and shortcuts;
- continually evaluate the reasonableness of their intermediate results; and
- repeat the process of statistical reasoning in a variety of contexts.

Modeling and Using Tools Practice Cluster (Practices 4 and 5)

Students use multiple different tools (e.g., rulers, counters, base-ten blocks, calculators) in the primary mathematics classroom. How the tools are used depends on the mathematics topic of focus, and the same tool might be used in a variety of contexts. When given a problem, students need to be able to determine what tool would be appropriate, how the tool could be used in solving the problem, and how to communicate about their process. In the early grades, students often use tools to model a problem. It is also important for students to be able to communicate about the modeling process by representing the process using numbers and symbols.

Mathematical Practice 4. Model with mathematics. Students demonstrate proficiency with this practice when they model real-life mathematical situations with a number or algebraic sentence or equation and check to make sure that their equation accurately matches the problem context. For example, students form expressions, equations, or inequalities from real-world contexts and connect symbolic and graphical representations. They begin to explore covariance and represent two quantities simultaneously. They use number lines to compare numbers and represent inequalities. They use measures of center and variability and data displays (e.g., box plots and histograms) to draw inferences about and make comparisons between data sets. Students use scatterplots to represent data and describe associations between variables. Students need many opportunities to connect and explain the connections between the different representations. They should be able to use all of these representations as appropriate to a problem context (CCSSO, 2010; Common Core Standards Writing Team, 2011–2012; North Carolina Department of Public Instruction, 2012a, 2012b, 2012c).

Students who model with mathematics are able to

- apply what they know to make approximations;
- identify important quantities in a problem situation;
- analyze relationships between quantities; and
- reflect on whether the results make sense.

Mathematical Practice 5. Use appropriate tools strategically. Students demonstrate proficiency with this practice when they access and use tools appropriately. Students consider available tools (including estimation and technology) when solving a mathematical problem and decide when certain tools might be helpful. For example, students might draw pictures, use applets, or write equations to show the relationships between the angles created by a transversal. They may decide to represent figures on the coordinate plane to calculate area. Number lines are used to understand division and to create dot plots, histograms, and box plots to visually compare the center and variability of the data. Additionally, students might use physical objects or applets to construct nets and calculate the surface area of three-dimensional figures (CCSSO, 2010; Common Core Standards Writing Team, 2011–2012; North Carolina Department of Public Instruction, 2012a, 2012b, 2012c).

Students who use appropriate tools strategically are able to

- consider available tools when solving a mathematical problem;
- make sound decisions about when each of these tools might be helpful;
- explain their choice of a particular tool for a given problem; and
- detect possible errors by strategically using estimations.

Overarching Habits of Mind of Productive Thinkers Practice Cluster (Practices 1 and 6)

Productive disposition refers to the tendency to see sense in mathematics, to perceive it as both useful and worthwhile, to believe that steady effort in learning mathematics pays off, and to see oneself as an effective learner and doer of mathematics. Developing a productive disposition requires frequent opportunities to make sense of mathematics, to recognize the benefits of perseverance, and to experience the rewards of sense making in mathematics. (NRC, 2001, p. 131)

Mathematical Practice 1. Make Sense and Persevere in Solving Problems. Students demonstrate proficiency with this practice when they make sense of the meaning of the task and find an entry point or a way to start the task. Students solve real-world problems involving ratio, rate, area, and statistics through the application of algebraic and geometric concepts. Students use concrete manipulative, pictorial, and symbolic representations as well as mental mathematics. Students also are expected to persevere while solving tasks; that is, if students reach a point in which they are stuck, they can think about the task in a different way and continue working toward a solution. They may check their thinking by asking themselves, "What is the most efficient way to solve the problem?" "Does this make sense?" and "Can I solve the problem in a different way?" They develop visualization skills connected to their mathematical concepts as they recognize the existence of, and visualize, components of three-dimensional shapes that are not visible from a given viewpoint (CCSSO, 2010; Common Core Standards

Writing Team, 2011–2012; North Carolina Department of Public Instruction, 2012a, 2012b, 2012c).

Students who use appropriate tools strategically are able to

- start by explaining to themselves the meaning of a problem and looking for entry points to its solution;
- make conjectures about a solution;
- plan a solution pathway rather than simply jumping into a solution attempt;
- monitor and evaluate their progress and change course if necessary;
- rely on using concrete objects or representations to help conceptualize and solve a problem;
- check their answers to problems using a different method;
- continually ask themselves, "Does this make sense?"; and
- make sense of the problem-solving approaches of others, noticing similarities and differences among approaches.

Mathematical Practice 6. Attend to precision. Students demonstrate proficiency with this practice when they are precise in their communication, calculations, and measurements. Students continue to refine their mathematical communication skills by using clear and precise language in their discussions with others and in their own reasoning. For example, students become more precise when attending to attributes, such as describing a triangle, square, or rectangle, as being *closed* figures with *straight* sides. They state precisely the meaning of variables they use when setting up equations, including specifying whether the variable refers to a specific number, or to all numbers in some range. During tasks involving number sense, students consider if their answer is reasonable and check their work to ensure the accuracy of solutions. When measuring or using measurement data, students attend to the unit (CCSSO, 2010; Common Core Standards Writing Team, 2011–2012; North Carolina Department of Public Instruction, 2012a, 2012b, 2012c).

Students who attend to precision are able to

- communicate precisely to others;
- use clear definitions in discussion with others and in their own reasoning;
- state the meaning of the symbols they choose, including using the equal sign consistently and appropriately; and
- specify units of measure to clarify the correspondence with quantities in a problem.

Learn more about how the Probes support teachers in assessing ideas related to the mathematical practices in Chapter 7.

Appendix B

Developing Assessment Probes

Developing an assessment Probe is different from creating appropriate questions for comprehensive diagnostic assessments and summative measures of understanding. The Probes in this book were developed using a process similar to that described in *Mathematics Curriculum Topic Study: Bridging the Gap Between Standards and Practice* (Keeley & Rose, 2006; Mundry, Keeley, Tobey, & Carroll, 2012). The process is summarized as follows:

- Use national standards to examine concepts and specific ideas related to a topic. The national standards used to develop the Probes for this book are Common Core State Standards for Mathematics (CCSSO, 2010). The Common Core Standards for Mathematics (referred to as CCSSM) define what students should understand and be able to do in K–12 mathematics.

- Within a CCSSM grade-level expectation, select the specific concepts or ideas you plan to address, and identify the relevant research findings. The sources for research findings include the *Research Companion to Principles and Standards for School Mathematics* (NCTM, 2003), *Elementary and Middle School Mathematics: Teaching Developmentally* (Van de Walle et al., 2013), articles from NCTM's *Journal for Research in Mathematics Education, Second Handbook of Research on Mathematics Teaching and Learning* (NCTM, 2007), and additional supplemental articles related to the topic.

- Focus on a concept or a specific idea you plan to address with the Probe, and identify the related research findings. Keep the targeted concept small enough to assess with a few items because Probes are meant to be administered in a short amount of time. Rather than trying to target as much information about a topic as possible it is better to be more narrow and focused.

- Choose the type of Probe format that lends itself to the situation (see more information on Probe format in Chapter 1's "What Is the Structure of a Probe?" beginning on page 13). Develop the stem (the prompt), key (correct response), and distractors (incorrect responses derived from research findings) that match the developmental level of your students.
- Share your assessment Probe(s) with colleagues for constructive feedback, pilot with students, and modify as needed.

Feedback on the assessment Probes developed for this resource was collected from 6–8 educators across multiple states, and the Probes were piloted with students across multiple grade levels. The feedback and student work were used to revise the Probes and to support the development of the accompanying Teacher Notes.

Appendix C

Action Research Reflection Template

QUEST Cycle

Questions to Consider About the Key Mathematical Concepts

What is the concept you wish to target? Is the concept at grade level or is it a prerequisite?

Uncovering Student Understanding About the Key Concepts

How will you collect information from students (e.g., paper and pencil, interview, student response system, etc.)? What form will you use (e.g., one-page Probe, card sort, etc.)? Are there adaptations you plan to make? Review the summary of typical student responses.

*E*xploring Excerpts From Educational Resources and Related Research

Review the quotes from research about common difficulties related to the Probe. What do you predict to be common understandings and/or misunderstandings for your students?

*S*urveying the Prompts and Selected Responses in the Probe

Sort by selected responses and then re-sort by trends in thinking. What common understandings/misunderstandings did the Probe elicit? How do these elicited understanding/misunderstandings compare to those listed in the Teacher Notes?

*T*eaching Implications and Considerations

Review the bulleted list and decide how you will take action. What actions did you take? How did you assess the impact of those actions? What are your next steps?

References

Ashlock, R. B. (2006). *Error patterns in computation.* Upper Saddle River, NJ: Pearson.

Askew, M., & Wiliam, D. (1995). *Recent research in mathematics education 5–16.* London, UK: HMSO.

Bay Area Mathematics Task Force. (1999). *A mathematics sourcebook for elementary and middle school teachers.* Novato, CA: Arena Press.

Black, P., & Harrison, C. (2004). *Science inside the black box: Assessment for learning in the science classroom.* London: NFER/Nelson.

Black, P., Harrison, C., Lee, C., Marshall, B., & Wiliam, D. (2004). Working inside the black box: Assessment for learning in the classroom. *Phi Delta Kappan, 86*(1), 8–21.

Bright, G., Joyner, J., & Wallis, C. (2003). Assessing proportional thinking. *Mathematics Teaching in the Middle School, 9*(3), 166–172.

Burns, M. (2005). Looking at how students reason. *Educational Leadership: Assessment to Promote Learning, 63*(3), 26–31.

Chapin, S. H., & Anderson, N. C. (2003, April). Formal proportional reasoning. *Mathematics Teaching in the Middle School, 8*(8), 420–425.

Chappell, M. F., & Thompson, D. R. (1999). Perimeter or area? Which measure is it? *Mathematics Teaching in the Middle School, 5*(1), 20–23.

Choppin, J. M., Clancy, C. B., & Koch, S. J. (2012). Developing formal procedures through sense making. *Mathematics Teaching in the Middle School, 17*(9), 552–557.

Circello, J. E., & Filkins, S. R. (2011). A new perspective on three-dimensional geometry. *Mathematics Teacher, 105*(5), 340–345.

Common Core Standards Writing Team (CCSWT). (2011a). *Progressions documents for the common core math standards, Draft 6–8, Progression on expressions and equations.* Retrieved from http://ime.math.arizona.edu/progressions/#products

Common Core Standards Writing Team (CCSWT). (2011b). *Progressions documents for the common core math standards, Draft 6–7, Progression on ratios and proportional relationships.* Retrieved from http://ime.math.arizona.edu/progressions/#products

Common Core Standards Writing Team (CCSWT). (2011c). *Progressions documents for the common core math standards, Draft 6–8, Progression on statistics and probability.* Retrieved from http://ime.math.arizona.edu/progressions/#products

Common Core Standards Writing Team (CCSWT). (2011d). *Progressions documents for the common core math standards, Draft 6–8, Progression on expressions and equations.* Retrieved from http://ime.math.arizona.edu/progressions/#products

Common Core Standards Writing Team (CCSWT). (2012). *Progressions documents for the common core math standards, Draft K–5, Progression on Geometry.* Retrieved from http://ime.math.arizona.edu/progressions/#products

Council of Chief State School Officers (CCSSO). (2008). *Attributes of effective formative assessment.* Retrieved from http://www.ccsso.org/Resources/Publications/Attributes_of_Effective_Formative_Assessment.html

Council of Chief State School Officers (CCSSO). (2010). Implementing the *common core state standards.* Retrieved from http://corestandards.org

Driscoll, M. (1999). *Fostering algebraic thinking.* Portsmouth, NH: Heinemann.

DuFour, R., DuFour, R., Eaker, R., & Many, T. (2006). *Learning by doing: A handbook for professional learning communities at work.* Bloomington, IN: Solution Tree.

Fosnot, C., & Dolk, M. (2001). *Young mathematicians at work: Constructing number sense, addition, and subtraction.* Portsmouth, NH: Heinemann.

Garcia, L. (2012). *How to get students talking! Generating math talk that supports math learning.* Retrieved from http://www.mathsolutions.com/documents/How_to_Get_Students_Talking.pdf

Giannakoulias, E., Souyoul, A., & Zachariades, T. (2005). *Students' thinking about fundamental real numbers properties.* Fifth Congress of the European Society for Research in Mathematics Education (17–21 Feb. 2005) in Larnaca, Cyprus.

Gregg, J., & Gregg, D. (2007). A context for integer computation. *Mathematics Teaching in the Middle School, 13*(1), 46–50.

Hannula, M. S. (2003). Locating fraction on a number line. In N. A. Pateman, B. J. Dougherty, & J. Zilliox (eds.), *Proceedings of the 27th Conference of the International Group for the Psychology of Mathematics Education,* Vol. 3, 17–24.

Hartweg, K. (2011). Representations and rafts. *Mathematics Teaching in the Middle School, 17*(1), 40–47.

Heritage, M. (2010). *Formative assessment: Making it happen in the classroom.* Thousand Oaks, CA: Corwin.

Institute for Mathematics and Education, University of Arizona. (2007). *Progressions documents for the common core math standards: About this project.* Retrieved from http://math.arizona.edu/~ime/progressions/

Kahlid, M., Rosmah, B., & Badarudin, H. (2012). *Using the jar model to improve students' understanding of operations on integers.* Presentation by J. Suffolk & B. Darussalem. Retrieved from tsg.icme11.org/document/get/874

Keeley, P. (2012). Misunderstanding misconceptions. *Science Scope, 35*(8), 12–13.

Keeley, P., & Rose, C. (2006). *Mathematics curriculum topic study: Bridging the gap between standards and practice.* Thousand Oaks, CA: Corwin.

Keeley, P., & Rose Tobey, C. (2011). *Mathematics formative assessment: 75 practical strategies for linking assessment, instruction and learning.* Thousand Oaks, CA: Corwin.

Lamon, S. J. (2006). *More: In-depth discussion of the reasoning activities in "teaching fractions and ratios for understanding"* (2nd ed.). Mahwah, NJ: Lawrence Erlbaum Associates Publishers.

Langrall, C. W., & Swafford, J. (2000). Three balloons for two dollars: Developing proportional reasoning. *Mathematics Teaching in the Middle School, 6*(4), 254.

Larson, M., Lott Adams, T., Fennell, F., Dixon, K., & Kanold, T. (2012). *Common core mathematics in a PLC at work.* Bloomington, IN: Solution Tree.

Loucks-Horsley, S., Love, N., Stiles, K., Mundry, S., & Hewson, P. (2003). *Designing professional development for teachers of science and mathematics.* Thousand Oaks, CA: Corwin.

Malloy, C. E. (1999). Perimeter and area through the van Hiele model. *Mathematics Teaching in the Middle School, 5*(2), 87–90.

McCallum B. (2011, March 10). Structuring the mathematical practices [Web log post]. Retrieved from http://commoncoretools.me/2011/03/10/structuring-the-mathematical-practices/

McTighe, J., & O'Connor, K. (2005). Seven practices for effective learning. *Educational Leadership: Assessment to Promote Learning, 63*(3), 10–17.

Mestre, J. (1989). *Hispanic and Anglo students' misconceptions in mathematics.* Charleston, WV: Appalachia Educational Laboratory. Retrieved from ERIC database (ED313192).

Moss, C., & Brookhart, S. (2012). *Learning targets: Helping students aim for understanding in today's lesson.* Alexandria, VA: Association for Supervision and Curriculum.

Mundry, S., Keeley, P., Rose Tobey, C., & Carroll, C. (2012). *Facilitator's guide to mathematics curriculum topic study.* Thousand Oaks, CA: Corwin.

National Council of Teachers of Mathematics (NCTM). (1993). *Research ideas for the classroom: Middle grades mathematics.* New York: MacMillan.

National Council of Teachers of Mathematics (NCTM). (1999). *Algebraic thinking.* Reston, VA: Author.

National Council of Teachers of Mathematics (NCTM). (2000). *Principles and standards for school mathematics.* Reston, VA: Author.

National Council of Teachers of Mathematics (NCTM). (2003). *Research companion to principles and standards for school mathematics.* Reston, VA: Author.

National Council of Teachers of Mathematics (NCTM). (2007). *Research on students' thinking and reasoning about averages and measures of center.* Reston, VA: Author.

National Research Council (NRC). (2001). *Adding it up: Helping children learn mathematics.* Washington, DC: National Academies Press.

National Research Council (NRC). (2005). *How students learn mathematics in the classroom.* Washington, DC: National Academies Press.

Naylor, S., & Keogh, B. (2000). *Concept cartoons in science education.* Sandbach, UK: Millgate House Education.

North Carolina Department of Public Instruction. (2012a). *NC common core instructional support tools: Math unpacking standards: Kindergarten.* Retrieved from http://www.ncpublicschools.org/acre/standards/common-core-tools/#unmath

North Carolina Department of Public Instruction. (2012b). *NC common core instructional support tools: Math unpacking standards: 1st grade.* Retrieved from http://www.ncpublicschools.org/acre/standards/common-core-tools/#unmath

North Carolina Department of Public Instruction. (2012c). *NC common core instructional support tools: Math unpacking standards: 2nd grade.* Retrieved from http://www.ncpublicschools.org/acre/standards/common-core-tools/#unmath

Parameswaran, R. (n.d.). Students' understanding of irrational numbers. Proceedings of epiSTEME 4, India. Retrieved from http://episteme4.hbcse.tifr.res.in/proceedings/strand-ii-cognitive-and-affective-studies-of-stme/parameswaran/view

Ponce, G. A. (2007). It's all in the cards: Adding and subtracting integers. *Mathematics Teaching in the Middle School, 13*(1), 10–17.

Resnick, L. (1983). Mathematics and science learning: A new conception. *Science, 220,* 477–478.

Rose, C., & Arline, C. (2009). *Uncovering student thinking in mathematics, grades 6–12: 30 formative assessment probes for the secondary classroom.* Thousand Oaks, CA: Corwin.

Rose, C., Minton, L., & Arline, C. (2007). *Uncovering student thinking in mathematics: 25 formative assessment probes.* Thousand Oaks, CA: Corwin.

Rose Tobey, C., & Minton, L. (2011). *Uncovering student thinking in mathematics grades K–5: 25 Formative assessment probes for the elementary classroom.* Thousand Oaks, CA: Corwin.

Ryan, J. & Williams, J. (2007). *Children's Mathematics 4–15*. Berkshire, UK: Open University Press.

Shaughnessy, M. M. (2011). Identify fractions and decimals on a number line. *Teaching Children Mathematics, 17*(7), 428–434.

Siegler, R., Carpenter, T., Fennell, F., Geary, D., Lewis, J., Okamoto . . . Wray, J. (2010). *Developing effective fractions instruction for kindergarten through 8th grade.* NCEE 2010-4039. Retrieved from http://ies.ed.gov/ncee/wwc/practice-guide.aspx?sid=15

Small, M. (2009). *Good questions: Great ways to differentiate mathematics instruction.* New York: Teachers College Press.

Stepans, J. I., Schmidt, D. L., Welsh, K. M., Reins, K. J., & Saigo, B. W. (2005). *Teaching for K–12 mathematical understanding using the conceptual change model.* St. Cloud, MN: Saiwood.

Tillema, E. S. (2012). What is the difference? Using contextualized problems. *Mathematics Teaching in the Middle School, 17*(8), 472–478.

Tobey, C. R., & Fagan, E. R. (2013). *Uncovering student thinking about mathematics in the common core, grades K–2: 20 formative assessments.* Thousand Oaks, CA: Corwin.

Van de Walle, J. A. (2007). *Elementary and middle school mathematics: Teaching developmentally.* Boston, MA: Allyn & Bacon.

Van de Walle, J. A., Karp, K., & Bay-Williams, J. (2013). *Elementary and middle school mathematics* (8th ed). Boston, MA: Pearson.

Watson, B., & Konicek, R. (1990). Teaching for conceptual change: Confronting children's experience. *Phi Delta Kappan, 71*(9), 680–684.

Wiggins, G., McTighe, J., & Association for Supervision and Curriculum Development. (2005). *Understanding by design,* expanded 2nd ed. Alexandria, VA: Association for Supervision and Curriculum. Retrieved from http://www.ascd.org/publications/books/103055/chapters/understanding-understanding.aspx

Wiliam, D. (2011). *Embedded formative assessment.* Bloomington, IN: Solution Tree.

Wylie, E., Gullickson, A. R., Cummings, K. E., Egelson, P. E., Noakes, L. A., Norman, K. M., & Veeder, S. A. (2012). *Improving formative assessment practice to empower student learning.* Thousand Oaks, CA: Corwin.

Yetkin, E. (2003). *Student difficulties in learning elementary mathematics.* ERIC Clearinghouse for Science Mathematics and Environmental Education. Retrieved from ERIC database (ED482727).

Index

CORWIN

A SAGE Company

The Corwin logo—a raven striding across an open book—represents the union of courage and learning. Corwin is committed to improving education for all learners by publishing books and other professional development resources for those serving the field of PreK–12 education. By providing practical, hands-on materials, Corwin continues to carry out the promise of its motto: **"Helping Educators Do Their Work Better."**